WOODWORKING with Plastics

Dedication

To my wife, Susan, who has been my first and most important editor for 37 years now.

ISBN 978-1-4971-0594-2

Library of Congress Control Number: 2026936473

Shutterstock used: Copy.photography (plastics pile: front cover), Q-Studio (factory background: front cover), Towhidul tohu (scratch background: 1, 3), A-R-T-I Vector (abstract background: back cover, 2, 9, 10, 11, 23, 39, 104, 106, 125), Edinaldo (4), baitong333 (5), anmbph (9)

To learn more about the other great books from Fox Chapel Publishing, or to find a retailer near you, call toll-free at 800-457-9112 or visit us at www.FoxChapelPublishing.com.
We are always looking for talented authors.
To submit an idea, please send a brief inquiry to acquisitions@foxchapelpublishing.com.
Or write to:
Fox Chapel Publishing
903 Square Street
Mount Joy, PA 17552

Printed in China
First printing

WOODWORKING with Plastics

26 Simple Projects to Bring Plastics into Your Woodshop

RALPH BAGNALL

Table of Contents

Introduction

Template cutting on the router table is perfectly familiar to woodworkers. It is simply being used here on a part made of nylon.

I began working with plastics at a small company in New Hampshire back in 1988. There I learned how to cut, mill, glue, and form sheet plastics, making everything from deli stands and roll bins to coffee bean dispensers. We used a lot of specialized equipment and tools designed specifically for plastics, but I was surprised to see how many of the "typical" woodworking tools I already knew were perfectly suited to plastic work.

In 2016 I created a seminar entitled "Plastics in the Woodshop" that I presented at the International Woodworking Fair (IWF) in Atlanta, Georgia. Since then, I have presented versions of that seminar at other shows. The keen interest I saw in this topic at these professional shows was also mirrored in the many questions I saw about cutting and working plastics on various woodworking forums, websites, and groups.

With all this in mind, I proposed this book to Fox Chapel Publishing and you are reading the result. It is my fourth book with Fox Chapel, and I believe the first woodworking book published specifically on this topic. I hope that everyone will find something useful within.

You are unlikely to find yourself working plastics more than wood in your shop, but at one time or another, most woodworkers will look at using some form of plastics. It may be as simple as including a clear panel on a project, such as the pencil dispenser on page 8 or glazing a picture frame like in Chapter 2. We may think of plastics as being unworthy to be included in "high-end" projects, but creative woodworkers

PHOTO CREDIT: DARRYL JONES

The beauty and impact of this urn is only possible because the artist incorporated mundane plastic plumbing parts into the design.

PHOTO CREDIT: MENU SOLUTIONS (PATTERSON, NEW JERSEY)

Common plastic utility items can benefit from incorporating wood elements that enhance the value and allow customization.

know better. The turned vessel at left is a project of undeniable creativity and beauty that is fully dependent on PVC plumbing fittings. The lid can be opened and closed or permanently sealed as needed, but to include this feature in the design, the artist had to know how to work the plastic parts to fit his needs.

Those who make money in their woodshop as a full-time job or a side gig can greatly enhance their opportunities by using even simple plastic elements into the woodworking they already know. Bent acrylic sign holders are commonly seen on restaurant tables; combining this idea with a well-designed wooden base makes it more attractive and allows for choices in species and stain colors. The "table tent" at left is a perfect example of this, and the forming techniques from Chapter 6 will show you how to achieve it.

I have specifically excluded resin casting from this book, as that process can be very involved and is well covered in books by folks with much more experience than I have. Similarly, I did not include 3D printing projects because while they can certainly be of great value in the shop, they require unique equipment to make and need few if any woodworking tools once printed.

Like all my books, I have built the lessons around projects. I firmly believe that the context of a project enhances understanding of the skill or technique being presented. This book differs in that each chapter is based around techniques and skills that are common to working plastics.

PHOTO CREDIT: DANIEL QUIROZ (DAN THE MAKER MAN)

A simple cut-and-drilled acrylic panel allows the user to see the pencils as they are dispensed from this clever device.

PHOTO CREDIT: MIKE KOZIKOWSKI

3D prints like this sanding block are useful, but the programming and machines needed are outside the scope of this book.

For example, most plastic projects will require finishing the edges to one degree or another. Rather than repeating these steps for each project, projects started in the cutting or milling chapters may be continued as topics in the edge-finishing chapter. This book is less about you making the projects in the book and more focused on using the projects in the book to teach the techniques for your own projects. I hope you find it useful as you explore adding plastics to your woodworking skills.

—***RALPH BAGNALL***

Safety Issues with Plastics in the Woodshop

Generally speaking, you should observe the same safety rules working with plastics that you do working with wood and sheet goods. Burning plastics can release toxic fumes, but nothing being discussed in this book should result in actual combustion.

- Always wear safety glasses and hearing protection in your shop.
- Read, follow, and understand the manuals that come with your tools and machines.
- Avoid loose clothing that can get caught in machines, bits, or blades. NEVER wear gloves working with machinery.
- Keep long hair tied back or otherwise secured.
- Remove watches and jewelry that can get caught in machinery or tools.

Remember that your mind is your most important safety device. Be aware of the risks and work around them if needed. If a cut scares you, do not do it. There is always a jig, fixture, or different tool that can let you safely finish the task. You are your own safety equipment.

Note on Metric Conversions

Imperial and metric measurements are included throughout this book. Where needed, the conversions will be exact, but whenever possible, the conversions will be practical.

For example, the Scribe Wheel from Chapter 2.3 requires a 1" center hole to fit over a specific guide bushing, so it is written as **1"** (**25.4mm**); however, the outer diameter is not critical, so it can be written in a way that makes it easy for all users, such as **2"** (**50mm**). Where the actual blank sizes do not matter, they will be noted with the most reasonable metric equivalent. For example, **10"** (**250mm**) is easier to measure to than the more exact 254mm. I hope this makes the book more useful for all readers.

Basic Plastic Types

The term "plastics" is generic and covers many materials with a very wide range of properties. Plastics all start in pellet form that is then melted and injected into molds, cast, or rolled as sheets or extruded into strips.

There are two basic classes of plastic. The first is thermoset materials, which are generally melted then formed. The housing of your drill is almost certainly a thermoset plastic. Once cooled, these thermosets are difficult to reheat and bend or otherwise reform without grinding them into pellets that can be recycled. The second class are thermoform plastics, which can be reformed from the sheet, rod, or bar shapes that you buy them in. They can be heat softened for strip bending, to fit over a form, and stretched or twisted as needed. The trim panels around airplane and bus seats are often thermoformed plastic.

These are very basic categories and there are many exceptions. Each specific type of plastic listed in this section will have many variants that are formulated for different needs, from transparency to strength to electrical insulation. In this list and throughout this book, we will be focused on the basics of each type.

ACRYLIC

- Easy to find in common sizes.
- Typically transparent with good optical properties. A good substitute for glass.
- Brittle; can be chipped and cracked with impact.
- Low melting point; can be heat formed.
- Can be assembled using solvent cements.
- Learn more about acrylic plastic in Chapter 2.1.

The most common plastic you will use, acrylic is available in many sizes and colors.

MYLAR®/PET

- A film made from stretching molten PET (polyethylene terephthalate) over cool rollers. Cuts readily with knives and scissors.
- Mylar is available in thin sheets and thicker sheets. PET is available as rods.
- Can be made shiny and reflective or translucent.
- Does not glue well but can be heat sealed.
- Learn more about Mylar plastic in Chapter 1.3.

PET is a very commonly used plastic in food packaging, and Mylar is made from PET.

NYLON

- Translucent to opaque. Comes in white, off white, and black; can be colored.
- Several grades of hardness; often used in cutting boards and wear surfaces.
- Can be mechanically assembled; does not glue well.
- Can be thermally welded with special equipment.
- Learn more about nylon plastic in Chapter 3.1.

Nylon is available in many formulations to meet specific requirements.

POLYCARBONATE

- Typically transparent with good optical qualities.
- Highly impact resistant; good for guards and shields.
- Surface scratches easily and is UV sensitive.
- Low melting point; heat formable.
- Can be assembled using solvent cements. Mills well and can be drilled and tapped.
- Learn more about polycarbonate plastic in Chapter 3.2.

Impact-resistant polycarbonate looks a lot like acrylic except for the cut edges, which can show a blue tinge.

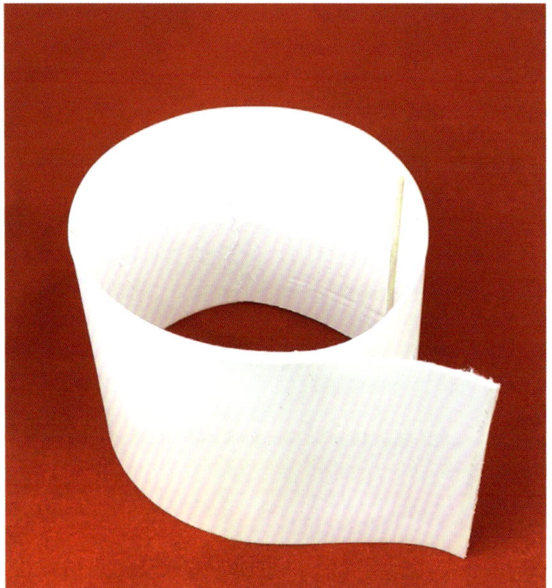

POLYETHYLENE /UHMW

- Available as thin drop cloths, sheets, rods, and bars.
- Translucent to opaque; not very see-through.
- Often used for food-grade products.
- Good friction and wear properties; used for glides and slides.
- Mechanical assembly only in the woodshop.
- UHMW (ultra high molecular weight) is a form of polyethylene. Has low surface friction and high wear resistance; protects surfaces that contact one another.
- Learn more about polyethylene plastic in Chapter 2.3.

Polyethylene is flexible and durable, so it is popular for rollers, guides, and slides.

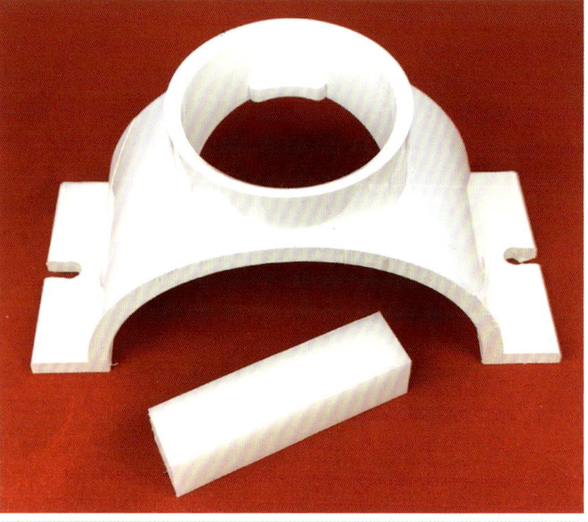

PVC

- Opaque in white, gray, and black.
- Most familiar as plumbing pipe but can come in block and sheet form.
- Solvent welds easily for assembly; can be mechanically fastened through drilling, tapping, and threaded inserts.
- Limited thermoforming capability.
- Learn more about PVC (polyvinyl chloride) plastic in Chapter 2.5.

Plumbing pipes and couplers are where PVC is encountered most, but it can be had in sheet and bar stock.

STYRENE/ABS

- Opaque, typically white or gray, in sheets and shapes.
- Easily thermoformed.
- Can be glued with solvent cements.
- Learn more about styrene and ABS (acrylonitrile butadiene styrene) plastic in Chapter 1.1.

Styrene is a component of ABS and is very popular for injection-molded parts.

Paper or Plastic?

Clear plastic sheets can be easily scratched, so they typically come with a protective film covering the faces.

Paper covers provide better protection but make it harder to tell what colors are underneath.

Acrylic and polycarbonate sheets always come with a cover sheet to protect the face from scratches and damage, while PVC and nylon-type plastics rarely have them. These sheets can be a clear plastic film or brown paper. Clear plastic film is the most common. These are applied as the plastic is made and generally are held in place by static cling. The film is easy to remove but does not protect the sheet very well because a scratch to the underlying plastic will readily cut through the film.

Paper is less common but does a much better job of protecting the face of the sheet. It is applied with a thin layer of rubber cement at the factory. Paper is reasonably easy to remove on new material, but it can become harder to peel cleanly after a few months on the shelf.

There is really little difference between paper and plastic covers except when milling plastics on a CNC machine. The paper stays on the sheet being cut, even with small parts. The film can sometimes come off and wrap around the router bit. When milling, I will typically leave paper film in place but remove the plastic film before cutting.

Chapter 1: Plastics That Can Be Worked with Craft Tools

Thin sheet plastics are easy to work with and very useful around the shop. They can be worked with common tools that any home will have, such as knives and scissors. Whatever sort of woodworking you do, these easy-to-find plastics will help improve your tools and projects.

1.1
SIMPLE STYRENE TEMPLATE

Sheet styrene is an excellent material for creating shop templates for scribing trim around thresholds and windowsills, creating repair fillers, and recreating custom moldings. Styrene sheets are easy to mark, cut, and shape. I recommend a model-grade styrene sheet, which you can find in craft and hobby stores or online. These are readily available in thicknesses from 0.005"–0.25" (0.1–6mm). Sheet styrene comes with a light matte finish, so pencils can mark it cleanly.

This chapter templates a section of molding that I need to match for a remodel. Having an accurate template allows for planning the tools needed and to check the results as we shape new parts.

Templates can be made as a "positive" model, like this one, which matches the part, or a "negative" version that fits into the shape of the stock being milled to check for accuracy. Make a positive first and label it to the job, source, or client as you need. If you do a lot of restoration, you will have a library of options that can be useful in the future. These "primary" templates can be used to create multiple copies of future templates that will all be the same since they share a source.

Simple templates have many uses around the shop when creating or reproducing moldings.

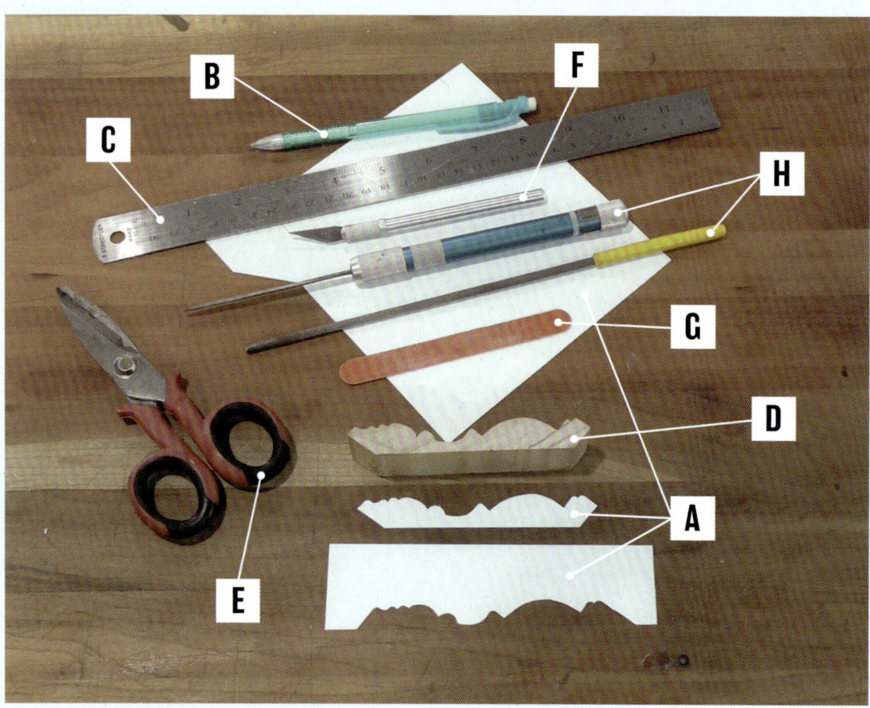

Sheet styrene is easy to work using common craft tools.

Supplies:

- **A.** Styrene sheet, 0.01"–0.03" (0.3–0.8mm) thick
- **B.** Pencil or mechanical pencil
- **C.** Ruler
- **D.** Molding or other piece to trace
- **E.** Scissors
- **F.** Utility knife
- **G.** Emery board or sandpaper
- **H.** Fine-tooth files (optional)

1. **Draw a baseline on the styrene.** Use 0.02"–0.03" (0.5–0.8mm) thick sheet of model-grade styrene for your templates. These will be stiff enough for checking your work while being easy to cut and shape with household tools. Draw a baseline near the edge of the sheet to reference your sample from. Mechanical pencils are ideal for this type of marking.

2. **Trace the piece on the styrene.** Hold the sample part firmly in place on top of the styrene sheet and trace the contour as close to the part as possible. Rotate the pencil as you work; this will keep the tip sharp as you use it. Don't worry about lines beyond the sample part; they will be removed as you cut out the profile. Samples taken from old sources may have been smoothed over time, be damaged, or have many coats of paint. Decide before cutting the template if you want to match these details to duplicate the existing molding in place or if you need to correct any defects for a restoration. This sort of template is suitable for marking and checking your work; it is not suitable for flush trimming at the router table.

3. **Use sharp scissors to cut most of the tracing out.** For inside sharp corners or tight curves, cut with a utility or hobby knife. Leave the pencil lines in place as you cut so you do not lose your reference. Check your cuts against the sample as you work to ensure accuracy—any defects here will be carried through onto whatever parts you make from this template. Fine-grit sandpaper, sanding sponges, and emery boards are all useful for fine tuning and smoothing the template.

Alternate Tools

Tools for paper, fabric, or leather are often well suited for use with thin sheet plastics. Punches like the one used in Chapter 1.2 can make circles as well as holes. The red-handled tool shown here, made by FastCap, is for making your own custom screw covers. Used with a common leather punch, they can make quick and easy washers or spacers from the same styrene and Mylar sheets being used in this book. Don't be afraid to experiment a little. You may already have a number of tools in your shop that will work quite well with plastics if you look for them.

Many paper and leather punching tools can be used with thin plastics.

4. **Cut the outline.** Use the "positive" template to choose the right type and size of router bits and shaper knives to reproduce the molding itself. Use it to mark out waste to be removed and to set up machines. I have also used this template technique to have custom router bits and shaper knives made for restoration projects.

1.2

STYRENE ROUTER FENCE SHIMS

Highly accurate metal shim stock is available, but it is too expensive and hard for many of us to work, especially as the stock gets thicker. Sheet styrene, ABS, or Mylar is an excellent alternative to steel for shimming fences, leveling table inserts, and similar general needs around the shop. The plastic sheet tolerances will not be as accurate as with steel but are accurate enough for most uses, such as this jointing shim set for your router table fence.

Styrene sheets come in common thicknesses that can make reasonably accurate shims.

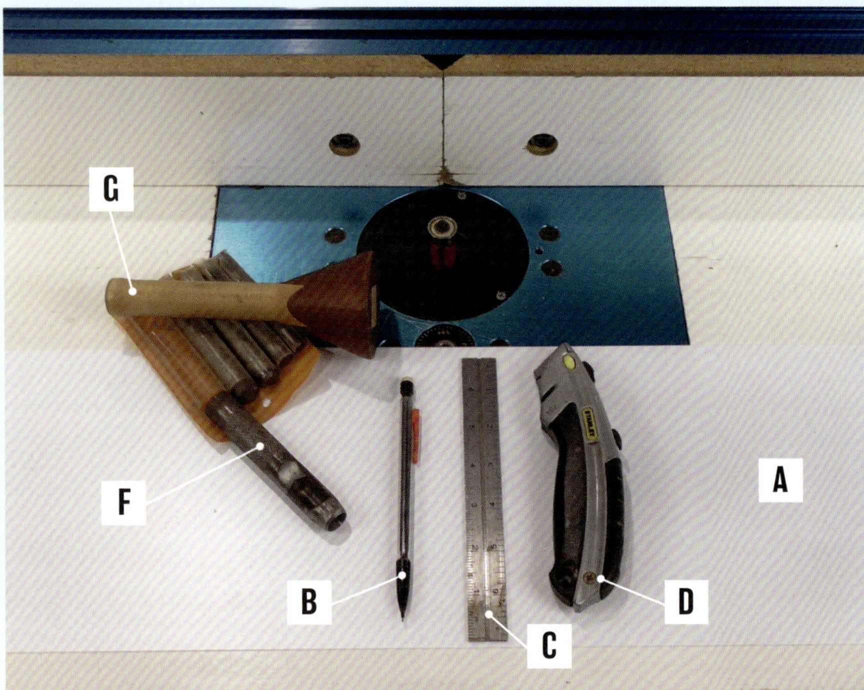

Complex shapes can be made with simple hand tools.

Supplies:

- **A.** Styrene sheet, 0.01"–0.08" (0.3–2mm) thick
- **B.** Pencil or mechanical pencil
- **C.** Ruler
- **D.** Utility knife or box cutter
- **E.** Sandpaper
- **F.** Hole punch (optional)
- **G.** Mallet or hammer
- **H.** Fine-tooth files (optional)
- **I.** Nylon cutting board (optional)

1. **Mark out the size of shim you need behind the outfeed fence of your router table.** It should be the same width and height as the fence face, with a bit extra along the top to serve as a handle. Measure and mark where any holes or slots need to go for the fasteners that secure the fence in place. The fence on my table uses two bolts, and I drew in two slots so the shim can be installed and removed by just loosening the fence face, not removing it. Two notches were also marked out along the top edge. Removing these will form the tab handle along the top of the shim. Your shim may need to have a different shape or other dimensions than what is shown depending on your router table fence design.

2. **Make the tops of your slots round.** Square corners are harder to cut neatly and are more likely to crack or tear than radius ones. Start cutting the slots by making a hole where the top of the slot will be. This can be done with a drill, but in these sheets, a hole punch is fast, accurate, and clean. The hardware on my fence is 1/4" (6.4mm), so I punch a 1/2" (13mm) hole to make it easier to align the shims during installation. I use an inexpensive nylon cutting board to back up the cut as I use the punch. Having a firm backer behind the punch will keep the edges of the hole from deforming as they are cut. They can be burnished flat if needed, but that is an extra step. Hold the punch square to the plastic and rap it sharply with a hammer to cut a clean hole. Punch circles for the notches that form the tab handle in the same way. Align the punch with lines drawn in step 1 so that the corner is cut round.

3. **Cut the slots and corners.** Align your ruler from the edge of the hole to the bottom of the shim and cut it using your utility knife. Do this for both sides of each hole, forming the slots. Cut the corners at the bottom of each slot round. This will also help make installing and removing the shims easier. Then use the knife to cut the lines forming the central tab. I chose to cut the vertical lines at an angle for a smoother look. Round all the other corners at the same time. These can be cut with a knife then lightly sanded to the final shape.

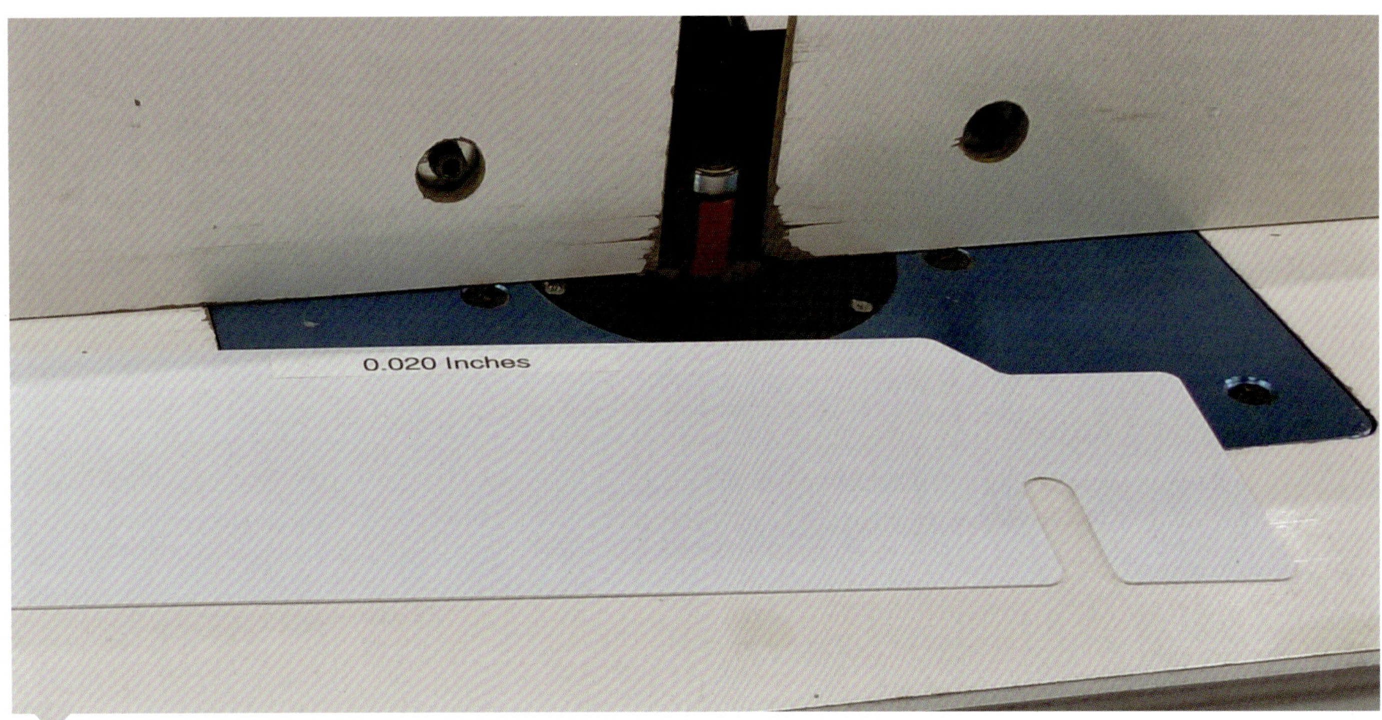

4. **Use this first shim as a template for making others if needed.** Trace the shape onto different thicknesses of plastic sheet and cut them the same way as in steps 1–3. Mark your shims for thickness to speed setup. Having a set of shims will allow you to adjust the offset of the router table fence based on your needs. For edging a board, I may use a stack of 0.06" (1.5mm) shims, but if I need to clean a plastic edge for polishing, I use a 0.03" (0.8mm) shim to just shave the saw marks off the edge.

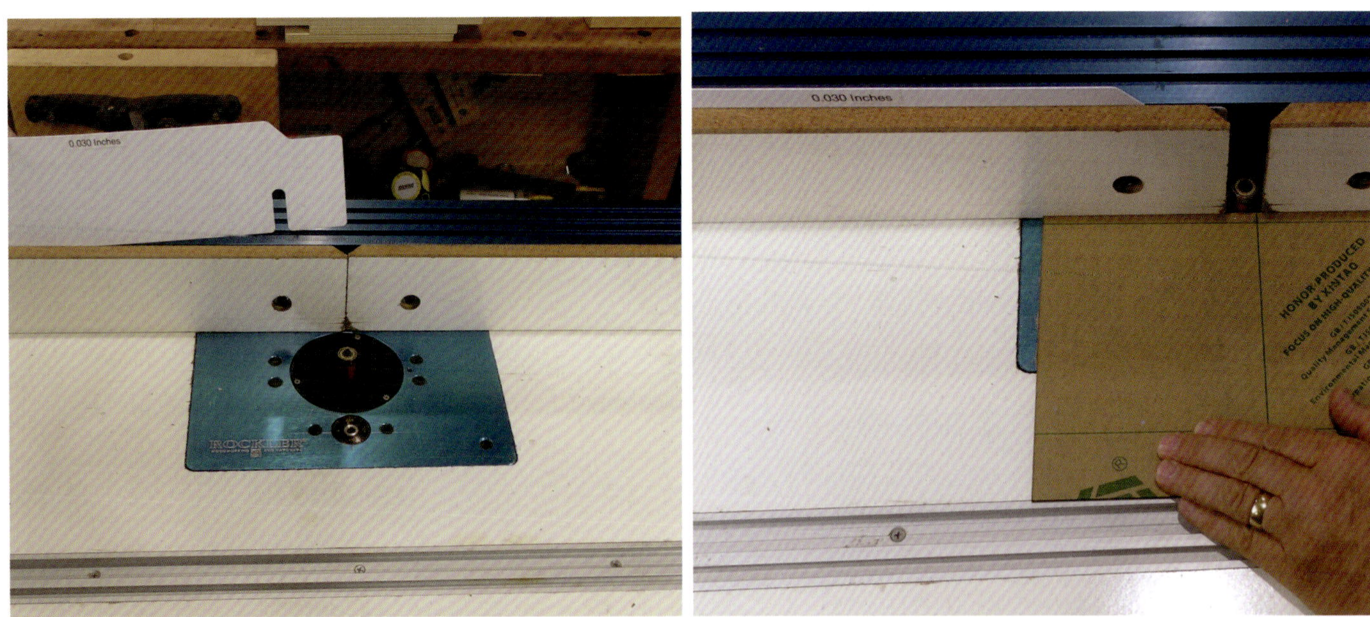

5. **Set up your router table as a jointer.** Install one or more shims behind the outfeed fence face of your router table and a straight cutting bit into the router. Use a straight edge to align the shimmed outfeed face with the cutting edge of the bit. The infeed face will be behind the cutter by the thickness of the shims you added. Add more shims for an aggressive cut and fewer shims for a finer cut. Edge joint your plastic or wood parts by feeding them from right to left across the router table. The bit will cut off the exact same width as the shims you stacked behind the outfeed fence. Here, I am removing 0.03" (0.75mm) to clean us a sawn edge for gluing or polishing.

Choose the Right Bit

Here I have installed Freud's 3/4" Diameter Downshear Helix Flush Trim Bit to use for jointing. The bit choice can make a difference. Larger diameter bits have a shallower cut angle than smaller diameter bits, and this shallow sweeping cut helps remove vibration and chatter when cutting. This bit also has the carbide mounted on the body at an angle, so it is considered a **helix** or **spiral** bit. The **shear angle** of these bits improves cut quality by slicing along an angle like a knife rather than chopping square against the edge like a chisel.

Bit choice can be important depending on the task.

1.3 MYLAR SKYLINE STENCIL

Most types of thin plastic sheet stock will work to make stencils, but Mylar is especially well suited for them. It is durable, flexible, and easy to clean between uses as needed. The smooth surface does mean that hand-drawn designs will need to be made with permanent marker rather than a pencil. These sheets are translucent enough to see a printed design through, making complex designs like the skyline in this project easier to cut.

Mylar sheets can be used to make durable, flexible, and easy-to-clean stencils for many projects.

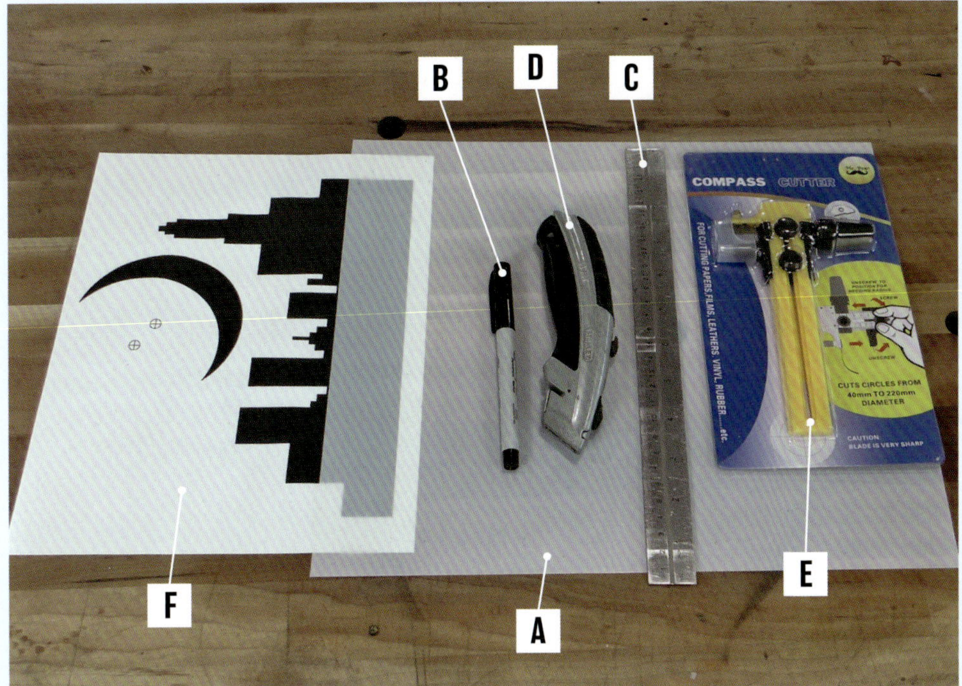

Mylar can be worked with the same simple craft tools as styrene.

Supplies:

- **A.** Mylar sheet, 6–10 mil (0.15–0.25mm) thick
- **B.** Fine-tip permanent marker
- **C.** Ruler
- **D.** Utility knife or box cutter
- **E.** Compass circle cutter (optional)
- **F.** Printed stencil template (optional)

1. **Print your design on paper and tape it to the underside of the Mylar sheet.** This allows you to work through the plastic without the template being in the way. A compass circle cutter can be adjusted to cut the moon outline easily. I created the drawing in a CAD program, so it was easy to mark the centers of the arcs that make up the moon. A pin holds the compass as it pivots, so the knife blade at the end of the arm cuts a perfect arc.

2. **Continue to cut the Mylar.** Depending on the complexity of the design, you can cut the Mylar by hand, with a ruler, or with a compass. This nighttime skyline stencil is made of mostly straight lines and regular curves; anyone can cut it out with a little care. The Mylar cuts easily and is tough enough not to tear even inside the small sections between the "buildings."

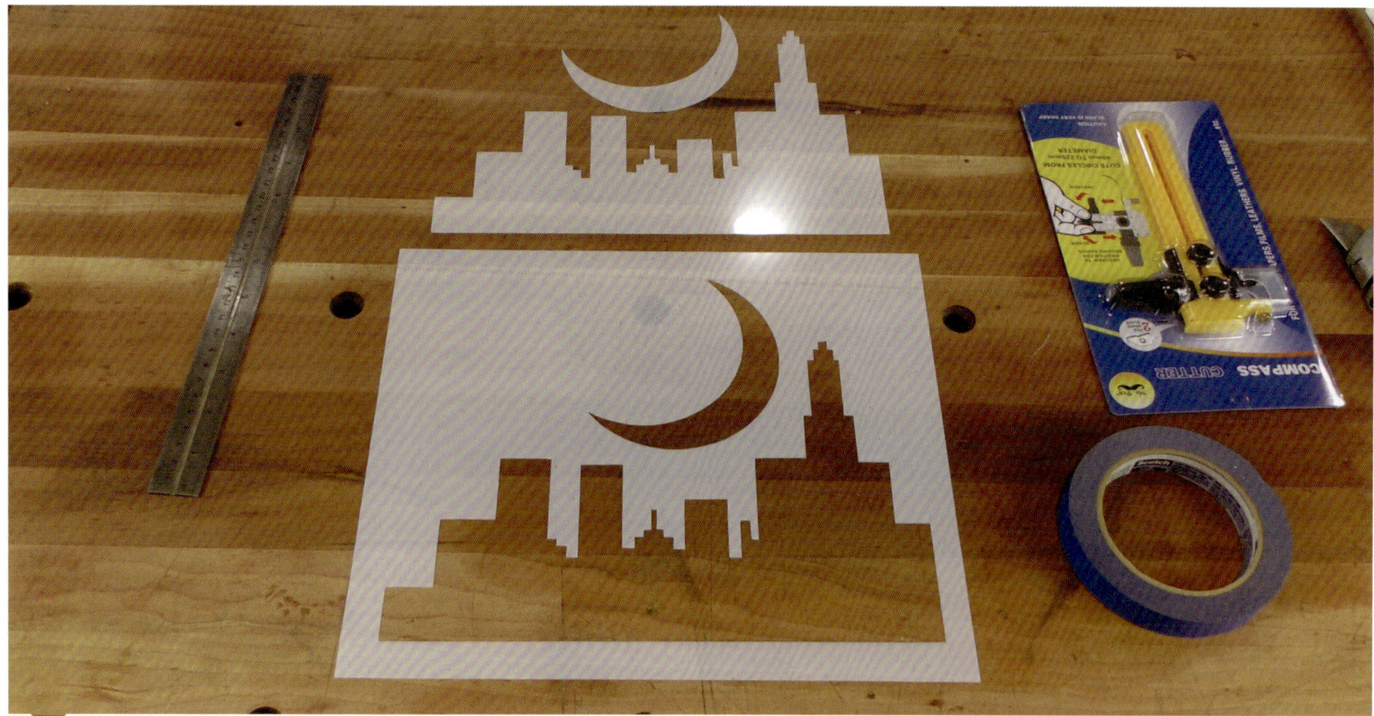

3. **Use the Mylar as a stencil.** You end up with both a negative stencil to apply paint only where the buildings are and a positive stencil to paint everything but the buildings. Both can be used for repeated patterns along wall borders, signs, plaques, and wall hangings. Stencils are just a durable mask to control where paint is applied. You do not need to be an artist to get great results.

1.4 JACK-O'-LANTERN STENCIL

For more complex stencil designs, such as this jack-o'-lantern, a digital cutting machine like the Silhouette or the Cricut used here lets almost anyone create their own designs. You can use clip art, draw your own images with your computer, or even scan a drawing and import it for cutting. This stencil can certainly be cut by hand, but if you happen to have a digital cutting machine, it is faster, easier, and allows for making many exact copies of even highly complex stencils.

Mylar is thicker than standard paper and tougher than cardstock. Be sure to check the manufacturer's specifications to see if your machine can cut Mylar and what settings to use.

Digital cutting machines make it easy to exactly reproduce stencils when needed.

Cutting machines are largely self-contained. You just need to add the material.

Supplies:

- A. Mylar sheet, 6–10 mil (0.15–0.25mm) thick
- B. Digital cutting machine
- C. Pick tools
- D. Spray paint
- E. Wooden pumpkin

Files for Cutting Machines

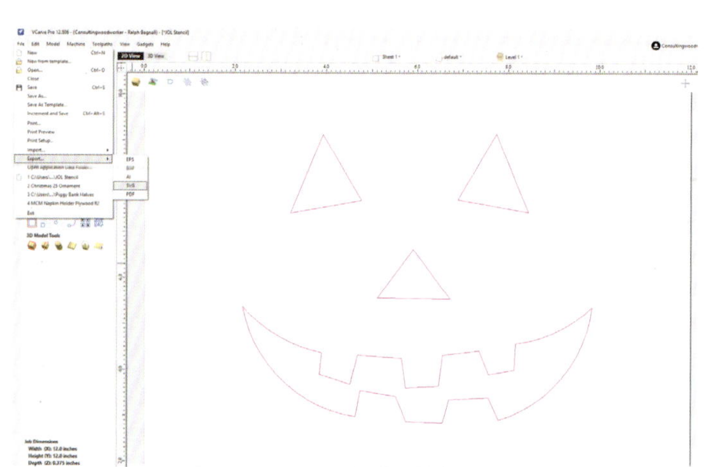
You can convert scans and images into usable .DXF or .SVG files in many CAD or graphics programs.

Cutting is easier working with CAD files rather than image files. You can use any number of graphics or CAD/CAM programs to trace images into files that the cutting machines can read, such as .DXF or .SVG. I use VCarve software for my CNC machines to convert the raster (image) files into vectors (CAD) that I save as .SVG files. Most CAD/CAM software packages have the ability to trace clip art, line drawings, and even photos into vector files that cutting machines can work with.

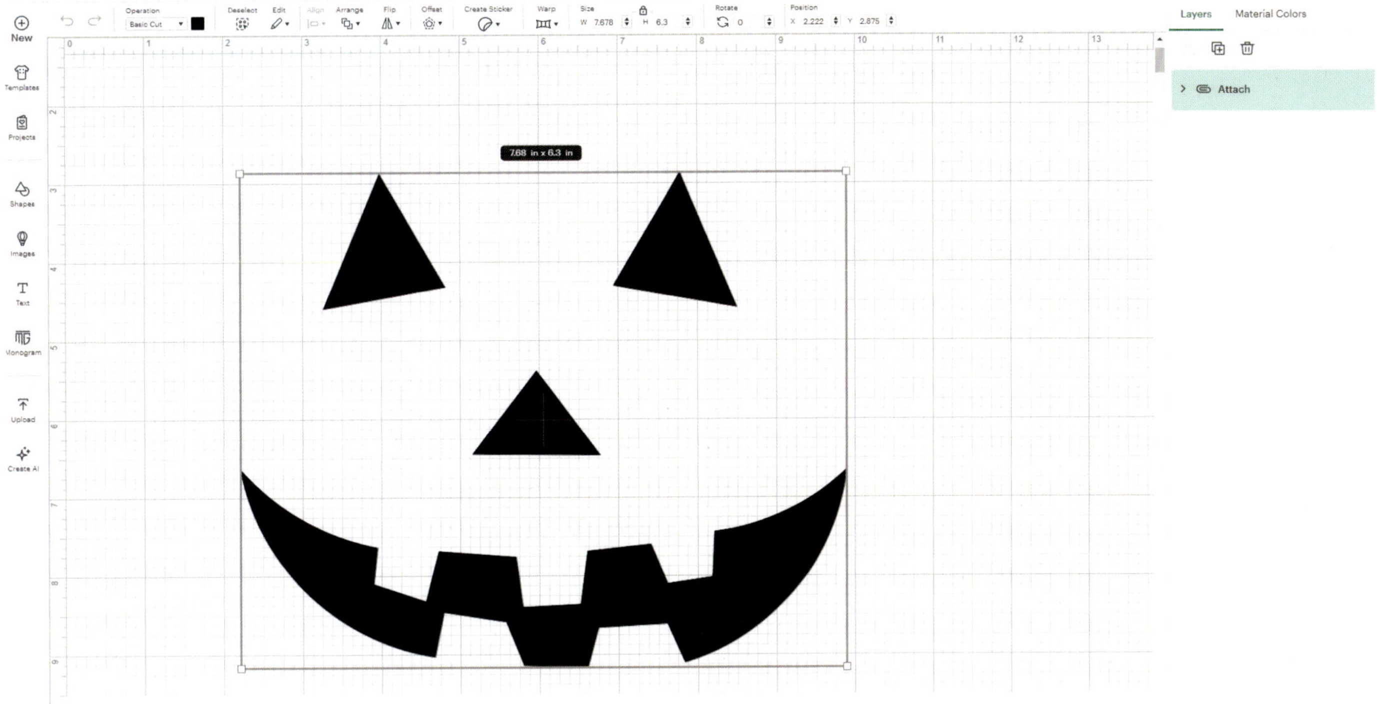

1. **Import your design into the cutting machine software.** The Cricut Design Space is shown here. The image can be sized, rotated, mirrored, and moved within the workspace. You can even combine separate drawings into a single project. The main limitation will be the sheet size the machine can cut.

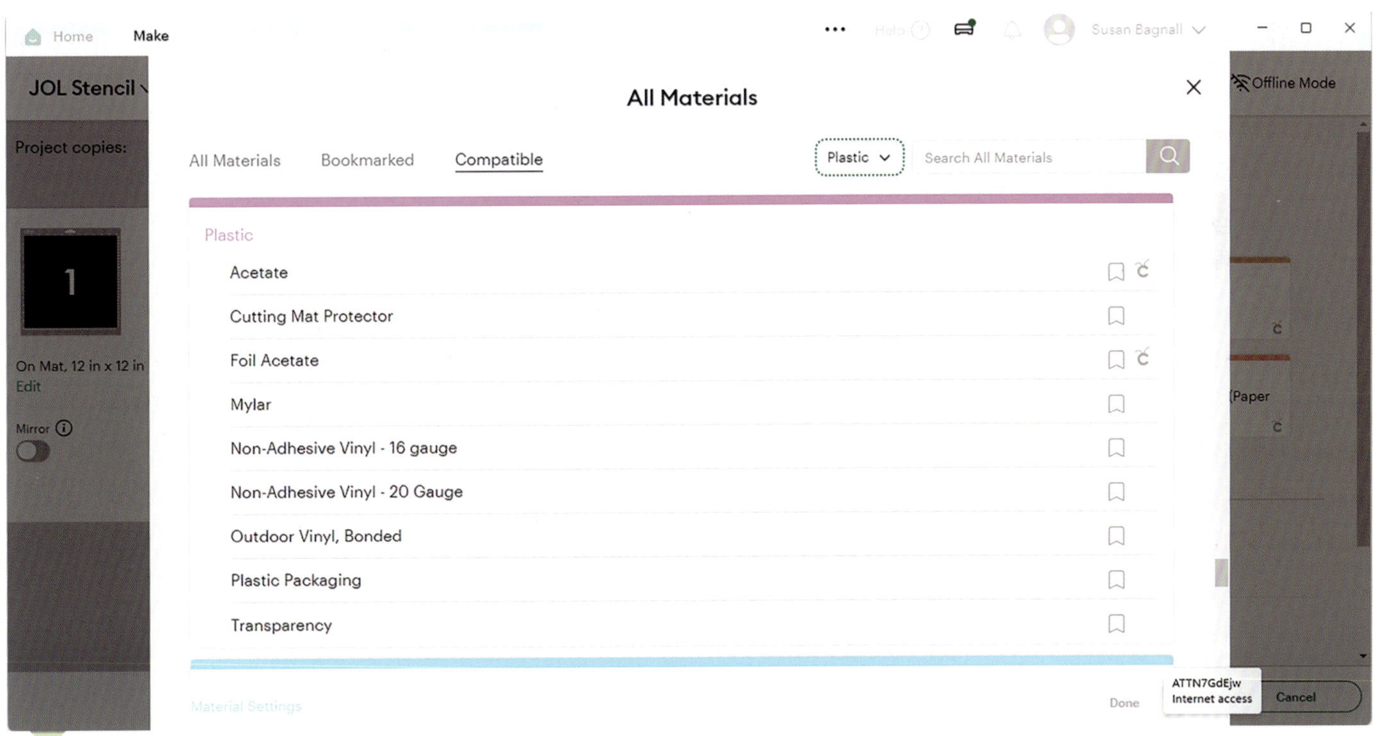

2. **Align the Mylar on the carrier sheet for the machine.** This carrier has a repositionable adhesive on it to hold the stock flat during cutting. It holds the stock to a known position within the machine to ensure that the cuts will be made in the right place. These carrier sheets come with different levels of tack to accommodate different materials. Be sure to follow the instructions for your particular machine. In the program, select the material to be cut. Mylar is one of the options with this machine, and there are also options for how deep to cut.

3. **Click on the run button once you have everything set up.** The Mylar may require a special blade or multiple cuts. These machines use a small drag knife to cut the stock. A drag knife is a small sharp blade that can swivel to follow the cut pattern. The tip of the knife is always slightly behind the center point of the head, so the machine may automatically over-cut corners a bit to produce the final pattern. This 7-mil Mylar did not cut through, even with two cuts being made by the knife. Simply running the program a second time separated all the parts fully.

4. **Peel the stencil off the carrier sheet.** With complex patterns, there may be several small parts that need to be removed. This is done with picks designed to help pull up the corners of the waste parts and to remove them from the sheet. Peel the body of the stencil off the carrier once the waste has been removed.

5. **Secure the stencil to the item you are marking or decorating.** This stencil is attached to a pumpkin shape that I cut on the bandsaw from a pine panel. It was painted orange and green and allowed to dry before stenciling. Spray paint through the stencil to complete the project. You will get the best results applying light coats until you get the coverage needed; excess paint can bleed under the edges of the stencil. Keep the can or sprayer square to the stencil and at enough distance to prevent the propellent from lifting the edges and getting under the stencil.

2

Chapter 2: Working with Thicker Plastics

Thicker plastics generally require different techniques than the simple ones outlined in Chapter 1 for thin sheets. They offer different challenges but are not difficult to work once you know the rules.

2.1

ACRYLIC GLAZING FOR ARTWORK

While glass is the typical material for glazing picture frames, acrylic is a great option for photos and artwork that may be hung in public spaces or around children. Acrylic is less likely to break into sharp, dangerous pieces should the frame be knocked off a wall or shelf. You can have plastic cut to size at a glass shop or hardware store when you purchase it, but thin acrylic is easy to cut to size even if you do not have a shop full of power tools. Buying stock-size sheets and cutting them yourself is more economical and easier to do. You don't even need a saw.

Plastic sheets of all thicknesses can be cut with various saws, but hard plastic sheets up to about 1/4" (6mm) thick can be sized using this score-and-snap technique without expensive tools—the scribing tool is inexpensive, and yardsticks are often free at hardware stores.

A simple shadow box with custom-sized acrylic glazing that the author cut by hand.

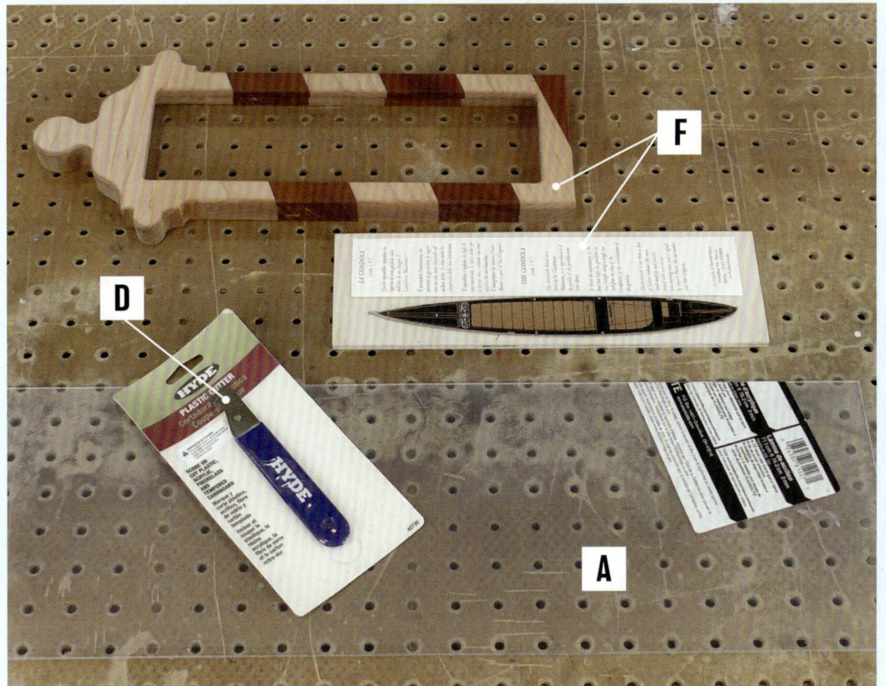

Very few tools are needed to cut thin acrylic sheets to size for many projects.

Supplies:

- **A.** Acrylic sheet, 0.03"–0.25" (1–6mm) thick
- **B.** Marker
- **C.** Ruler or other straight edge
- **D.** Scoring tool
- **E.** Utility knife
- **F.** Picture frame and artwork

1. **Measure your frame backer.** Your glazing should be the same size. The acrylic will come with a protective film on it, usually clear but sometimes paper; leave this in place as you work to protect the acrylic. Measure and mark the acrylic with a marker along the first measurement.

Scoring

Glass is not usually cut; it is scored along a line and snapped into two pieces. Acrylic works in much the same way. A score is made and the sheet is snapped along the edge of a bench or table. The scribing tool for scoring plastic is simple and inexpensive. It requires less technique than glass cutting, so it is also easier to do. The tool is a simple handle with a steel tip formed to a V-shaped point. The tool does not cut the plastic like a knife; instead, it is dragged along a straight edge so the tip scribes a V groove in the surface of the plastic. This V, like the line etched in glass, allows the plastic to break where wanted rather than simply shattering.

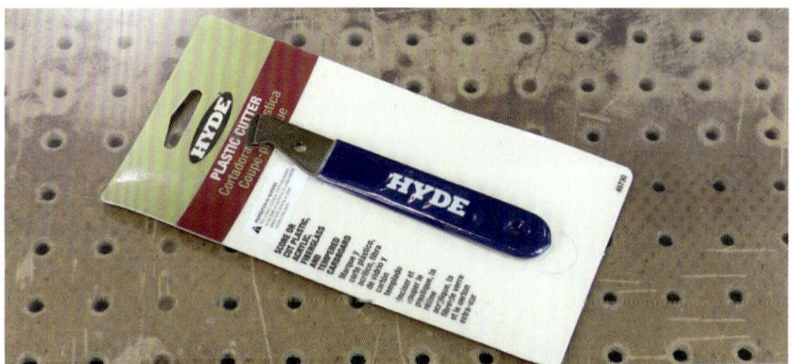

A variety of inexpensive scribe tools are available online, at hardware stores, and at home centers.

2. **Score the acrylic.** Set a straight edge along the cut line and use the scribing tool to score a line at the dimension needed. Hold the straight edge firmly as you score. Clamp it in place if it cannot be held easily; it is important to have only one score line to get a good break. Hold the tool firmly on the top of the acrylic sheet and pull it along the ruler from edge to edge. Score this line a few times on thicker sheets to ensure a clean break. The tool will scribe through the protective film, so there is no need to remove it.

3. **Align the score along the edge of a bench, table, or countertop.** Look for a square edge to snap against that will support the plastic along the break line. A smoothly rounded table edge is not suitable. Hold the sheet firmly on the surface and press down on the overhanging part quickly to break it along the score line. The film on the opposite side will still be connected to the rest of the plastic. Cut this with a sharp knife to keep it from peeling the protective layer off the remaining material.

4. **Mark and score any other cut lines needed and snap the acrylic to the final dimensions.** This "score-and-snap" technique can produce a pretty clean edge, and inside a picture frame, it will not be seen so often does not require much—if any—cleanup. If the edges do need some attention, lightly sand them or pass them over the jointer or router table to remove excess damage (see Chapter 4.1).

5. **Check the fit of the acrylic inside your frame.** Make sure it fits inside the back of the frame but not touching the outer edges. The acrylic will expand and contract differently than the frame, so the fit should not be too tight. If it fits, you can begin peeling the protective film off. Start by peeling the film from one side of the plastic only. This face will be inside the frame.

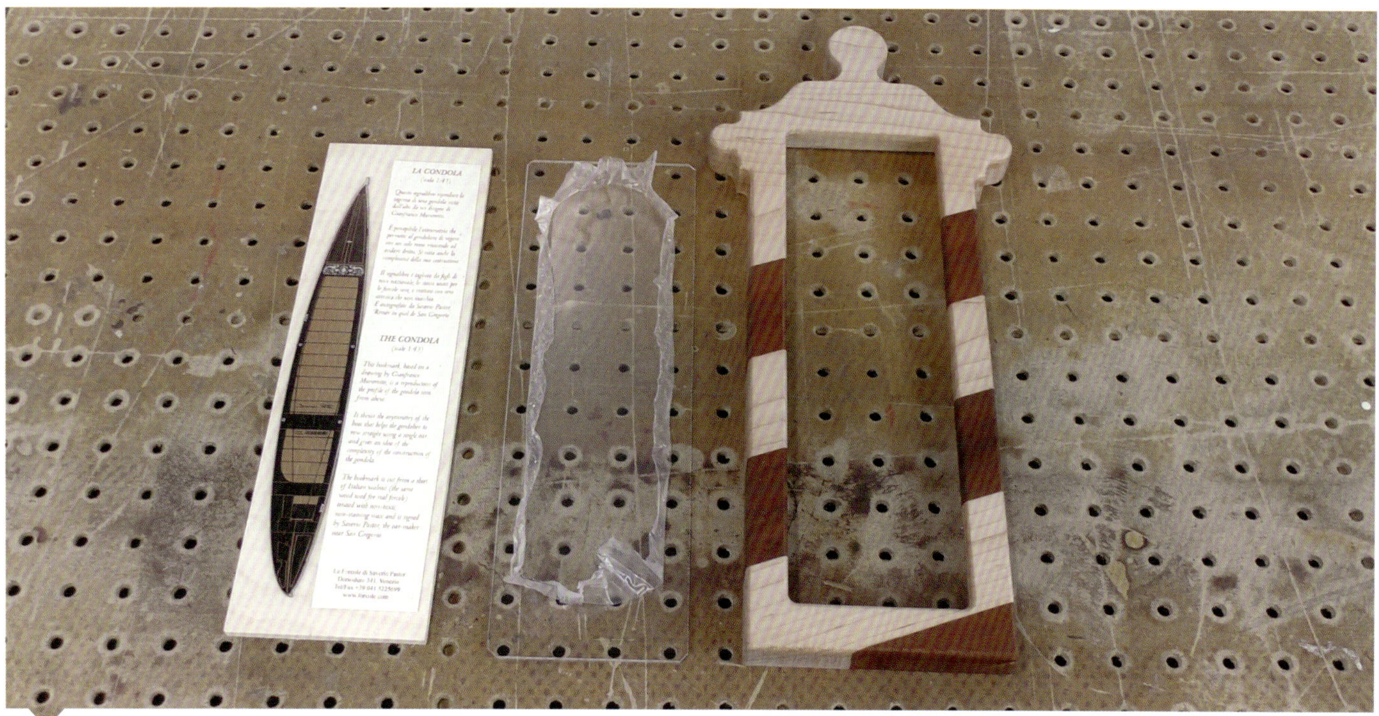

6. **On the other side, peel the film back along the edges.** Only go far enough so the film is not trapped in the frame as the acrylic is set in place. Leaving the film on will protect the plastic from dust and scratches as you continue to work. The peeling can cause static, which will attract dust, so make sure the face is clean before fitting it in the frame.

7. **Put it all together.** Set the acrylic into the frame, lay any matte in place, and set the artwork and the backer inside. Secure the backer into the frame with the clips that came with it or with frame points if you made your own frame, as used here. Peel the protective film off the front of the acrylic. Wipe it clean if there is any dust on it, and your frame is ready for display.

2.2

WINDOW HANGER BLANK

While the "score-and-snap" method from Chapter 2.1 is useful, cutting plastics to size using a table saw is faster, more efficient, and good for virtually all plastics of all thicknesses. Just like working with wood, each type of plastic will have specific issues to deal with when cutting, but vibration and heat are problems common to all plastics. The Skyline Silhouette artwork from Chapter 1.3 is an excellent opportunity to make your first saw cuts in acrylic. Make a blank here that can be paired with the stencil for a fun wall hanging.

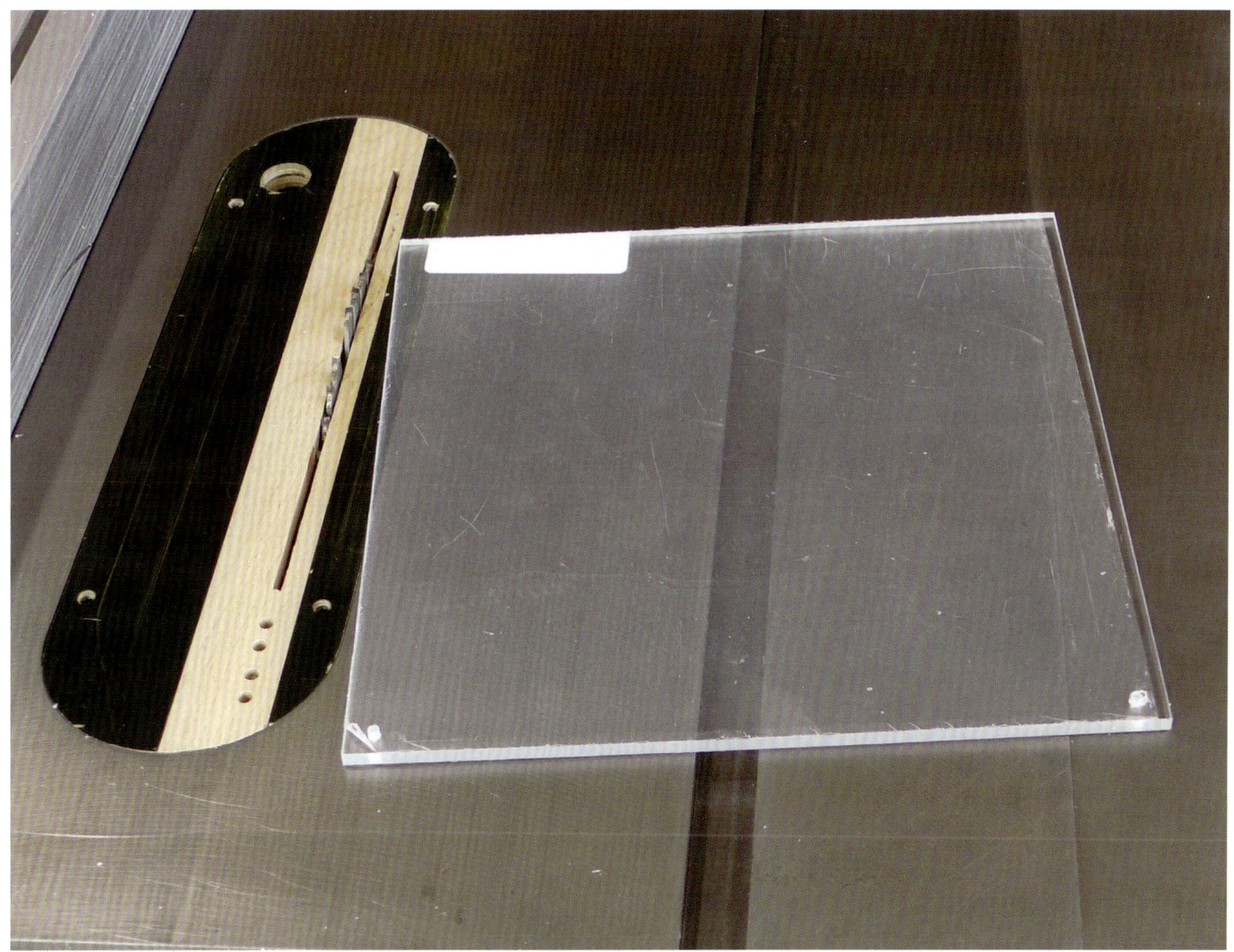

Use the table saw to cut thicker plastics when the score-and-snap method is not practical.

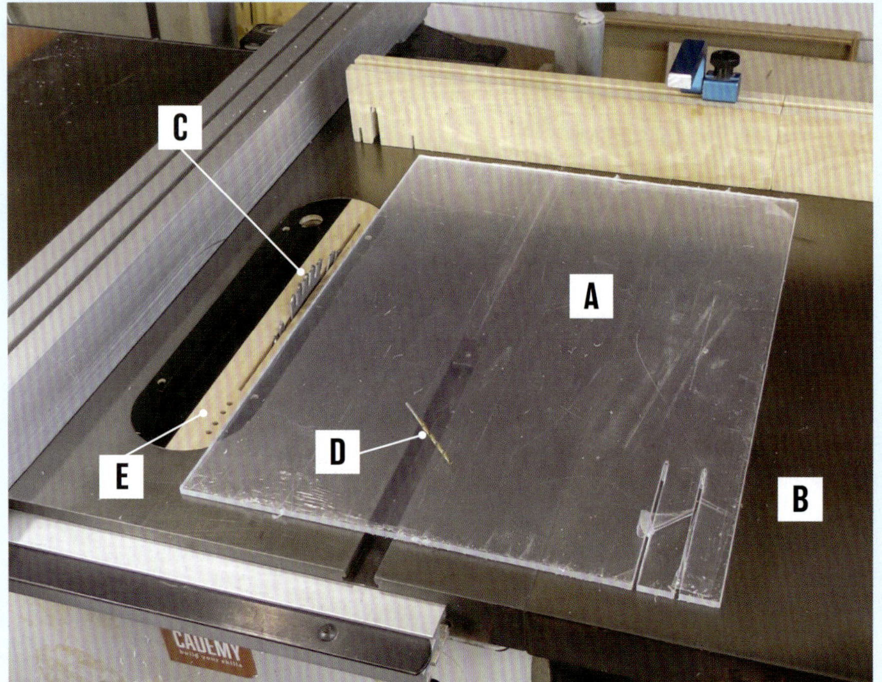

The right blade and a zero-clearance insert make short work of sizing your thicker plastic sheets.

Supplies:

- **A.** Acrylic sheet, 0.25" (6mm) thick
- **B.** Table saw
- **C.** 10" (250mm) ATB combination blade, 40–60 tooth
- **D.** 1/8" (3mm) twist drill bit
- **E.** Zero-clearance throat plate insert (optional)

1.

Dust off the top of the table saw. Remove any chips, dust, or other debris that might scratch the plastic as you cut. A clean workspace is even more important when working with plastics that can be scratched easily. Keep the protective film on the plastic whenever possible to protect the surface.

2.

Cut the acrylic sheet against the rip fence. Make 10" (250mm) wide cut using a zero-clearance insert and ATB combination blade. Keep the stock tight down on the saw table and push the plastic past the blade at a steady rate. Just as with wood, you want to push as fast as possible without bogging the saw down.

Blade Choice with Plastic

Understanding blade design can help you choose the right blade for your work.

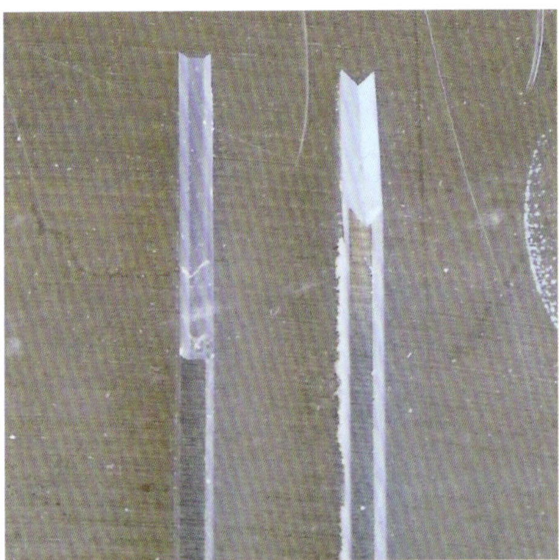

The additional teeth in the "fine-cut" blade only increase the friction heat during the cutting process.

An entire range of specialty saw blades is available just for processing plastics. Fortunately, woodshops that only need to occasionally cut plastics do not need to invest in specialty blades that will get little use. There is a common 10" (250mm) woodworking blade that works very well with virtually all plastics: the 40–60 tooth alternating top bevel (ATB) combination blade. Combination blades of this type are made by just about every manufacturer and are the basic blade type that comes with most saws. The alternating bevel teeth are designed to score the edges of the cut line first, then remove the waste in between. This works well for leaving clean sharp edges on any plastic being cut.

You may wonder why a fine-tooth blade would not cut better, especially in brittle plastics like acrylic, and the answer is heat. An 80-tooth crosscut blade, even with the ATB grind, is simply making too many contacts with the stock as it is cutting. Each contact between tooth and plastic generates friction heat, causing the plastic to melt along the cut line.

You can clearly see the difference in the two cuts shown at left. On the left is a cut made with a 40-tooth combination blade, and on the right, one made with an 80-tooth crosscut blade from the same manufacturer. Both are 10" (250mm), full kerf, and ATB ground, but the 80-tooth kerf clearly shows beads of plastic that have melted in the cut and rehardened along the edges of the kerf. These beads will need to be removed, and the edges of the part will not be clean. Fewer teeth are better here.

Dangerous Climbing

Thin stock climbing up the blade arc is dangerous and can lead to chipping and even breaking.

Supporting thin sheets on both sides of the cut requires some setup but is worth the effort.

Thin materials like laminates and veneers tend to flex and ride up the blade during cutting. Thin plastics are no different. When the stock is climbing the curve of the blade and a tooth engages the plastic above the table, the sheet can slam down onto the table, causing chips and cracks. While raising the blade can mitigate this issue somewhat, climbing can still occur and the excess blade exposure above the table poses a safety hazard.

The proper solution is holding the plastic tight to the table on both sides of the blade. Spring-loaded blade guards are one option for holding the sheets to the table. Another option is to use push blocks like MICROJIG's GRR-RIPPERs. These can be configured to pass over the blade with a leg on each side, keeping the stock firmly on the table as it passes the blade.

3. **Crosscut the strip.** Make another 10" (250mm) wide cut using the saw's miter gauge or a crosscut sled. Hold the plastic sheet on both sides of the cut if there is enough room. This will keep it from rising over the blade. An extended auxiliary fence is useful for pushing both pieces from the cut fully past the blade.

4. **Prep for finishing and hanging.** Drill a 1/8" (3mm) hole in the upper corners of the piece by hand or at the drill press, as shown here. Just make sure to hold the stock firmly on a clean backer under the bit to help prevent chipping at the exit point. These holes are to be used later for hanging. With the right blade, the edges of the plastic should be mostly clean with few tool marks. These will be finished in Chapter 4.1 to whatever level you want for your window hanger. Once the edges are finished, the stencil from Chapter 1.3 can be used to spray-paint the skyline silhouette onto the acrylic sheet.

2.3
VISE SOFT JAWS

Polyethylenes are a family of plastics that are used in everything from plastic bags to milk jugs to plastic forks, knives, and spoons. They are softer and less brittle than acrylics and are often used for low-friction applications, such as drawer slides. High-density polyethylene (HDPE) is a common choice for protective surfaces like these vise jaws. It is strong enough to take the forces applied in a heavy-duty machinist's vise without marking off on the wood or plastic parts being held.

These jaws require considerable milling—they will end up being 6" (150mm) x 1-1/8" (28mm) x 3/4" (19mm) to fit the vise shown. They feature a 3/4" (19mm) wide x 1/4" (6mm) deep rabbet along one face, which you can cut using either a table saw or a router table. Your vise may require different dimensions, but the parts may be hard to hold safely when milling.

Jaws can be made safely if the steps are organized to minimize risk. Most of the milling will be done while the jaws are still attached to the larger plastic blank for this reason.

Sometimes a softer touch is needed when holding parts. These jaws are easy to make and use.

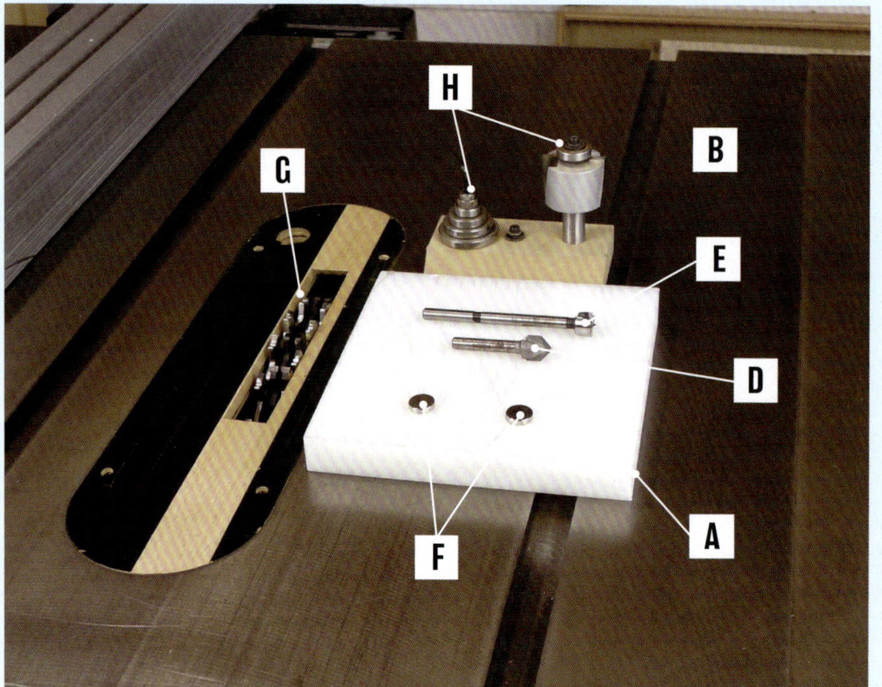

These jaws only require the most common of woodworking tools to make them.

Supplies:

- **A.** HDPE, 0.75" (19mm) thick x 6" (150mm) wide x 6" (150mm) long, or long enough to cover your vise jaw
- **B.** Table saw
- **C.** Router table
- **D.** 90-degree V-bit
- **E.** 1/2" (13mm) Forstner bit
- **F.** Four 1/2" (13mm) diameter magnets
- **G.** Stacked dado blade (optional)
- **H.** Rabbeting router bit (optional)

1a. Cut the rabbet on a table saw. Set a stacked dado blade in the table saw to full width, about 13/16" (20mm), and set the cut depth to 1/4" (6mm). Adjust the rip fence to cut a rabbet 3/4" (19mm) wide along the outside edge of the part. Cut this rabbet into both edges of the blank. If your setup cannot cut the full width in one pass, two passes can be made, adjusting the rip fence between cuts.

1b. Cut the rabbet on a router table. If you do not have a dado set or your saw cannot accept one, set up a rabbet bit or other flat cutter in the router table. Set up the router table to cut the rabbet against the fence, moving it back for as many passes as needed to make the full 3/4" (19mm) width. Cut the rabbet into both edges of the blank.

2. **Use a 90-degree V-bit at the router table to cut a groove along each jaw.** Set the bit to 1/4" (6mm) high and 1/2" (12mm) from the fence. This cut is along the length of the jaw and will be used for holding small, round, or odd-shaped parts. It is important to mill both jaws using the same setup so they match when mounted in the vise.

3. **Cut the jaws from the blanks at the table saw.** Set the rip fence so the jaw is cut from the blank on the far side from the rip fence. The finished jaw should be 1-1/8" (28mm) wide. The rabbet makes the jaw hard to hold properly, so cutting it on the off-fall side of the blade prevents kickback. Reset the rip fence to cut the second jaw from the blank in the same way.

4. **Notch the ends of the jaws at the router table.** This can be done using a miter sled on your table or sliding along the fence if your table does not have a miter slot. In either case, it is important to fully support the jaws as they are cut across the narrow side. The same bit setup as before is used, and again, it is important to ensure that the cuts match up to each other across the jaws.

5. **Drill mounting holes for the magnets.** These need to be positioned on the inside face of the rabbets cut at the beginning. They should be centered in the rabbet top to bottom, but be sure to check the side-to-side position. You want the magnets inside the vise jaws while avoiding any mounting screws or other obstructions on the factory jaws of your vise. The holes should be sized for the magnets. Adhesives are hard to use with magnets and nearly impossible with HDPE plastic, so a good press-fit is best. For 1/2" (13mm) magnets, I drilled 1/2" (12.7mm) holes. Test your bit and magnets on a scrap before drilling into your vise jaws.

6. **Attach the jaws.** They can be attached and removed from the vise pretty much instantly. The very slightly larger magnets fit snugly into the holes. The HDPE is just flexible enough to hold them firmly in place.

These jaws came in handy at many times when writing this book, such as clamping the napkin holder in Chapter 4.2

2.4

DRILL PRESS SCRIBE WHEELS

Router bits in a CNC are one of the best ways to cut circles and arcs in almost any plastic, but not having a CNC in your shop does not mean you can't make the items you need to. Hole saws are excellent when cutting circles in wood, but they have many teeth and no way of ejecting the cuttings, so they will quickly overheat your plastic and will not provide clean edges. In this case, one tooth is better than many. An adjustable circle cutter, like the one used here, is a very useful tool for not a lot of money. Chuck it in your drill press to make any number of useful items out of plastics (and wood), including the scribe wheels shown here.

These scribe wheels can be made with a small hole in the center to hold a pencil or marker. They are very useful when marking a countertop or wall scribe for cabinets. The scribe wheel here is designed to fit over a standard 1" (25.4mm) router guide bushing to add an additional 1/2" (12.7mm) offset for template routing. The offset allows cutting a shape from a glued-up blank using a standard guide bushing, then milling a juice groove using the same template.

Circles cut from plastics have many uses around the shop, from scribing for counters to a template offset like this one.

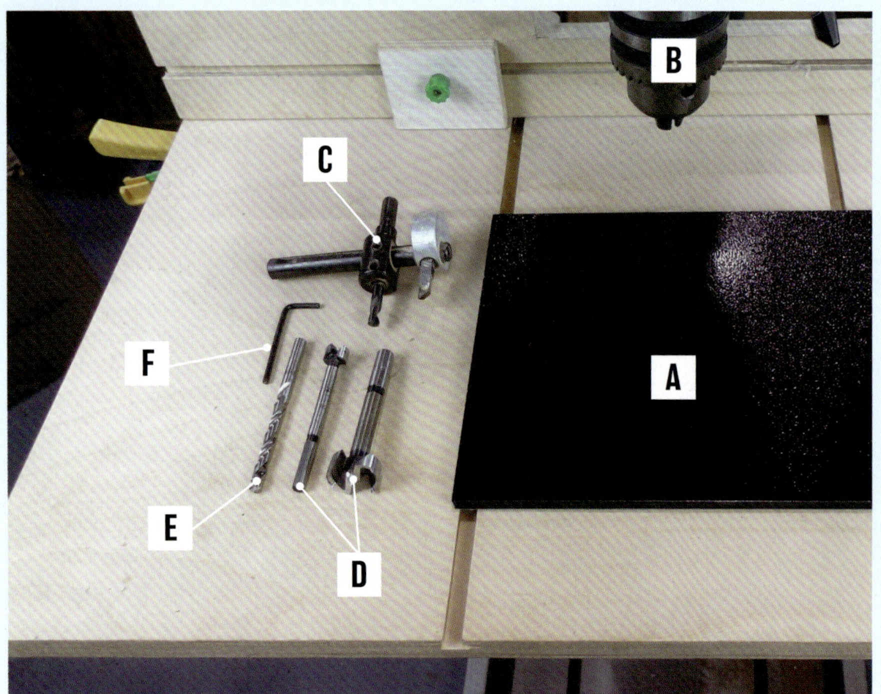

An inexpensive circle cutter in the drill press allows for making wheels or holes in plastic as well as wood.

Supplies:

- **A.** ABS or nylon sheet, 0.375" (9.5mm) thick
- **B.** Drill press
- **C.** Adjustable circle cutter
- **D.** Forstner bits
- **E.** 1/4" (6mm) twist drill bit
- **F.** Allen wrench
- **G.** Clamps

1. **Assemble your circle cutter as required.** The blade on the end of the arm can be set to cut a hole into a sheet or a circle out of a sheet. The difference is which edge is cut straight and which is angled like the cutter. Set the blade with the point to the inside of the arm to cut a wheel out of the plastic sheet. Adjust the length so the arm extends beyond the center to cut the required diameter. This scribe wheel needs to be 2" (50mm) in diameter, so set the arm 1" (25mm) from the center. Set the drill press to a low speed, 300 RPM if possible. Most drill presses have stepped pullies to allow for setting the RPM.

2. **Clamp the stock to the drill press table.** Set up so the circle cut is entirely within the plastic. This cutter is aggressive, and the arm extends beyond the work area, so clamping the stock in place improves both safety and cut quality. Start the drill press and lower the quill. The pilot bit in the center of the circle cutter will meet the plastic first. This acts as a center pin to keep the stock in position as the blade begins to cut the stock. Drill into the sheet stock, maintaining a firm pressure on the feed-arm. The goal is to cut as rapidly as possible without slowing the motor. If necessary, lift the cutter occasionally to clear the plastic shavings. Cut about halfway through the stock, then stop and raise the quill.

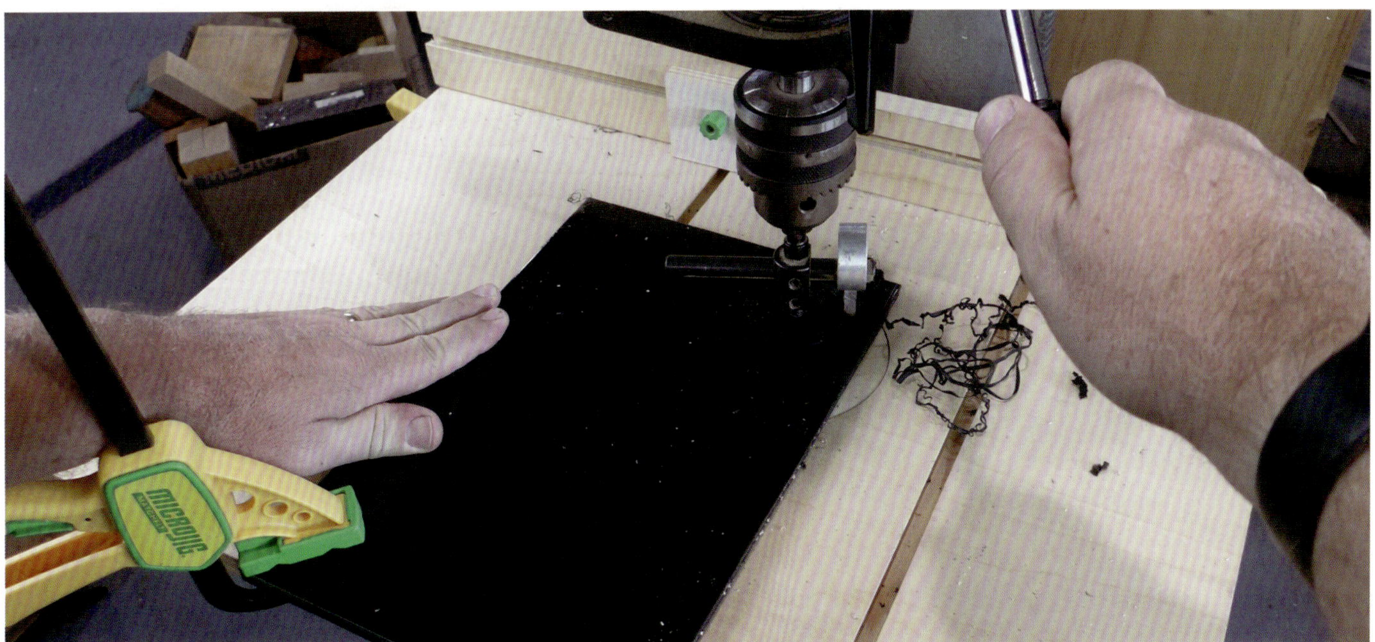

3. **Turn the sheet over and position it under the pilot bit.** With the drill press off, you can lower the circle cutter until the pilot bit fits into the center hole of the circle. Clamp the stock to the table and raise the quill back up. Start the drill press again and cut the plastic the rest of the way through. The plastic circle should come free as the blade reaches the previous cut on the underside. Making the cut from both sides improves the edge quality by eliminating much of the friction from the blade rubbing against the walls of the cut.

4. **Remove the circle from the sheet.** You now have a 2" (50mm) diameter circle with a 1/4" (6.4mm) pilot hole in the center. The pilot hole helps stabilize the part when cutting and is very useful for relocating the circle for further operations—like the 1" (25.4mm) hole this wheel needs in the exact center.

5. **Drill a new center hole.** Turn off the drill press and use a bit to relocate the newly cut circle under the quill. Set the fence and a stop block to record the right location, then clamp the circle in place or use double-face tape if it is small. Mount a 1" (25.4mm) Forstner bit into the chuck and drill through the center of the circle. Clamping is important here because the spur on the Forstner bit is in the pilot hole and cannot guide the bit.

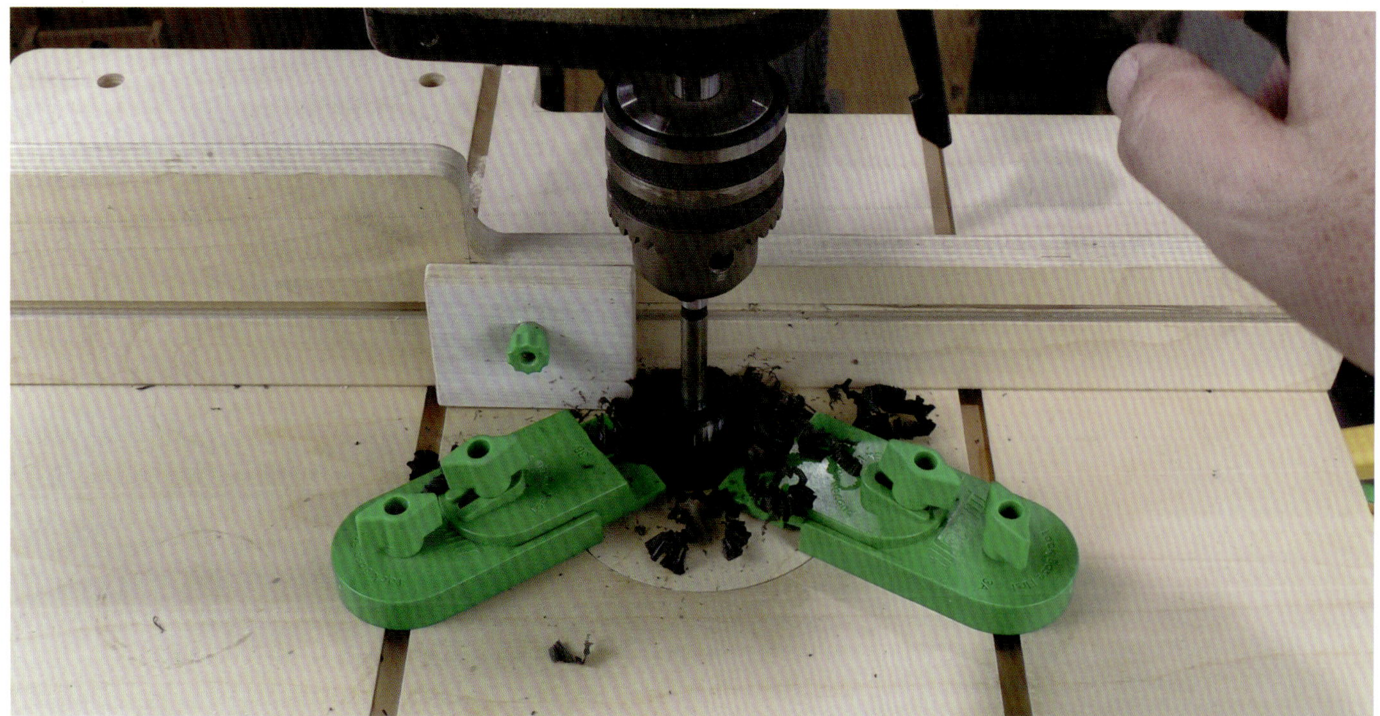

6. **Clean up the wheel.** Remove any burrs on the scribe wheel and relieve any sharp edges with sandpaper. The wheel is ready for use.

2.5

ROUTER TABLE DUST PORT

Heat buildup from friction is the major concern when cutting or milling plastics. Using the proper tools makes it easy to control the cutting conditions and attain the best results. This PVC saddle tee and a little hardware are an excellent starting point for making a custom dust port for the router table.

A saddle tee is a PVC plastic fitting you can buy at hardware stores and home centers. It is designed to add a new connection onto an existing 4" (101.6mm) PVC pipe. In the right size, it also makes an excellent dust port for your shop-built router table fences. PVC pipes and their fittings are easy to work with common tools and get excellent results. The odd shape of this part makes it ideal for working with the bandsaw or hand saws.

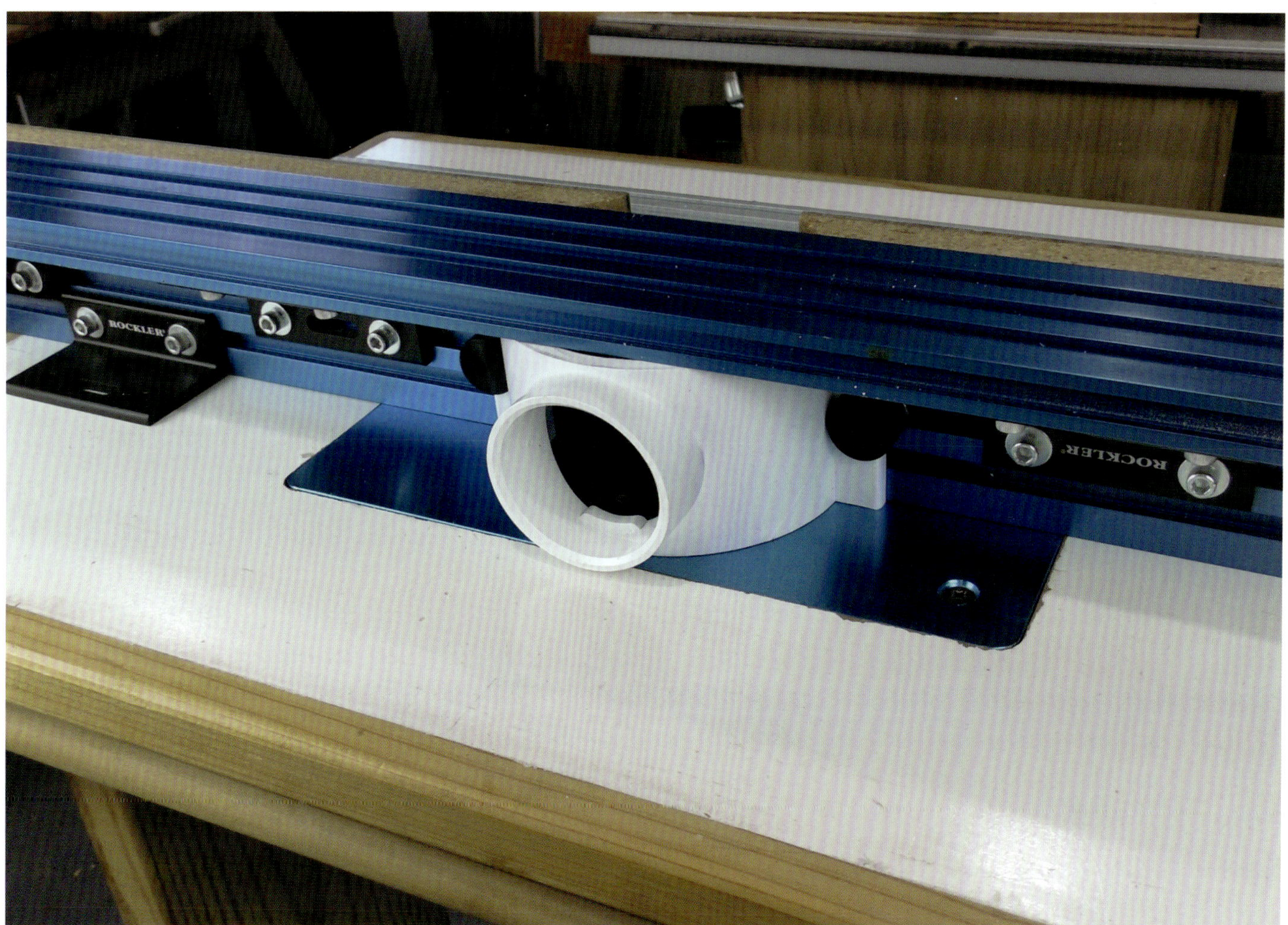

PVC plumbing fittings are often a good starting point for all sorts of dust collection needs around the shop.

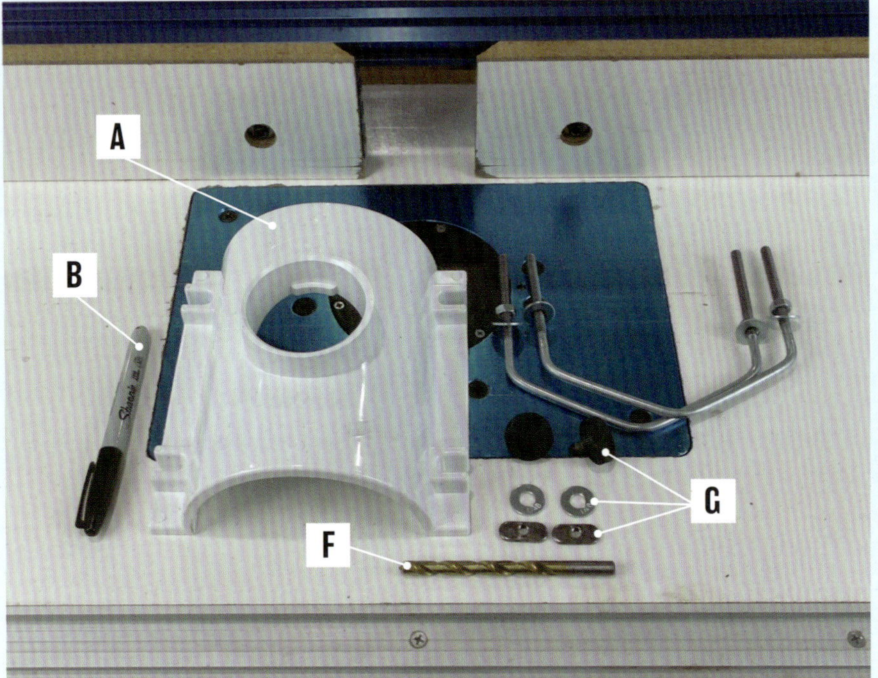

The right fittings and a few tools are all you may need to improve your shop dust collection.

Supplies:

- **A.** PVC saddle tee, 4" (101.6mm) x 2" (50.8mm)
- **B.** Marker
- **C.** Ruler
- **D.** Bandsaw
- **E.** Hand saw (optional)
- **F.** 5/16" (8mm) drill bit
- **G.** Mounting hardware

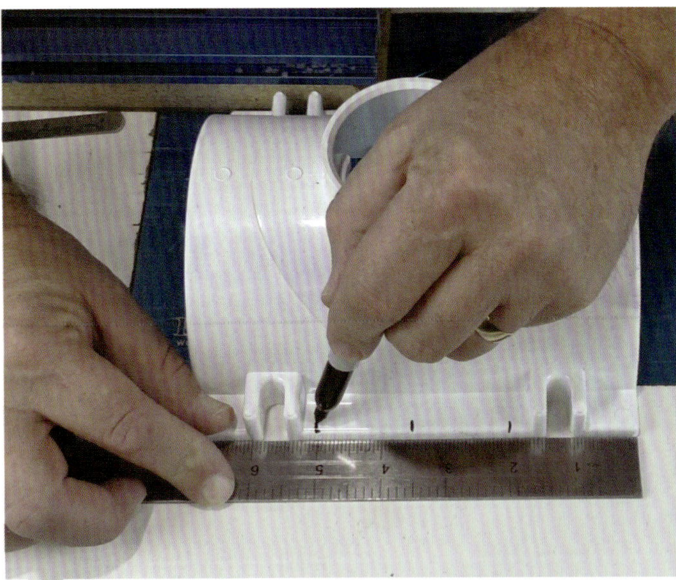

1. **Measure and mark the saddle tee where it needs to be cut to fit your fence opening.** Orient the saddle so the "tee" section is the connection for the vacuum hose and the 4" (101.6mm) arc becomes the chamber surrounding the bit. This router fence is 3" (76mm) under the top, so marks were made at the center point and 1-1/2" (38mm) to each side. These marks were then continued around the shape of the saddle tee.

2. **Cut the excess from each side of the 2" (50.8mm) opening.** The bandsaw makes quick work of this cut. The 1/2" (13mm) 7 TPI blade cuts fast and leaves a reasonably clean edge. The bandsaw teeth have plenty of time to cool as they travel around the wheels before cutting the plastic again, so melting is not an issue with straight cuts. Lacking a bandsaw, these cuts could easily be made with a good hand saw.

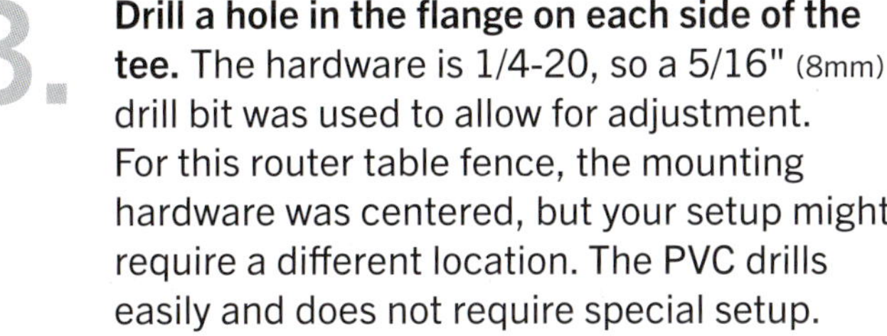

3. **Drill a hole in the flange on each side of the tee.** The hardware is 1/4-20, so a 5/16" (8mm) drill bit was used to allow for adjustment. For this router table fence, the mounting hardware was centered, but your setup might require a different location. The PVC drills easily and does not require special setup.

4. **Cut each mounting hole to the edge of the flange to form them into slots.** Slots are easier when removing and replacing the dust port in the confined space behind the fence. A simple hand saw makes quick work of this and is easy to control the exact cut line. File and sand any sharp edges as needed.

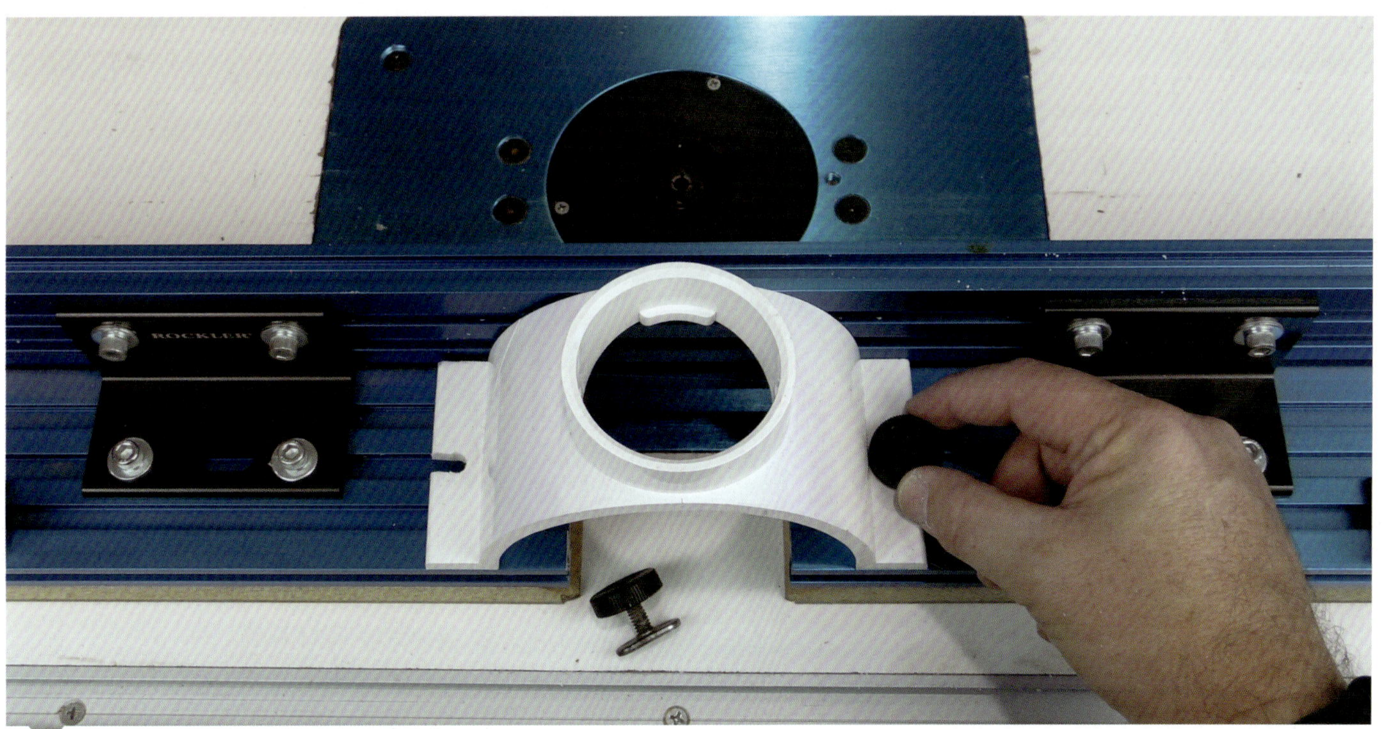

5. **Secure the dust port into place using the hardware needed for your fence.** The fence shown is made from extruded aluminum bar with T-tracks, so flat nuts were used with knobs. The opening on this saddle tee is 2" (50.8mm) inside, so if your hose does not fit inside the circle, you can glue in a short length of 2" (50.8mm) PVC pipe on which the hose can clamp to the outside. If your dust system uses a smaller hose, you can buy saddle tees in several configurations; just select the one that suits your needs best.

3

Chapter 3: Milling Plastics

Just like wood, working with plastics is about more than just cutting to size. Plastics can be drilled, grooved, shaped, and routed. The difference centers mostly around heat issues. The bits and blades used will be familiar to you, so great results can be had when using the right techniques.

3.1

SHOP-BUILT ROUTER BASE PLATE

The same 50-tooth ATB blade used for cutting acrylic in Chapter 2.2 will provide very clean cuts in softer plastics like nylon. I chose to use nylon since it is easy to work and soft enough that it won't scratch or mark even when cutting on finished surfaces. I have always found nylon to be highly useful around the shop for miter bars, drawer slides, push sticks, and router bases like the one I am making here, so my trim router can be fitted with a guide bushing.

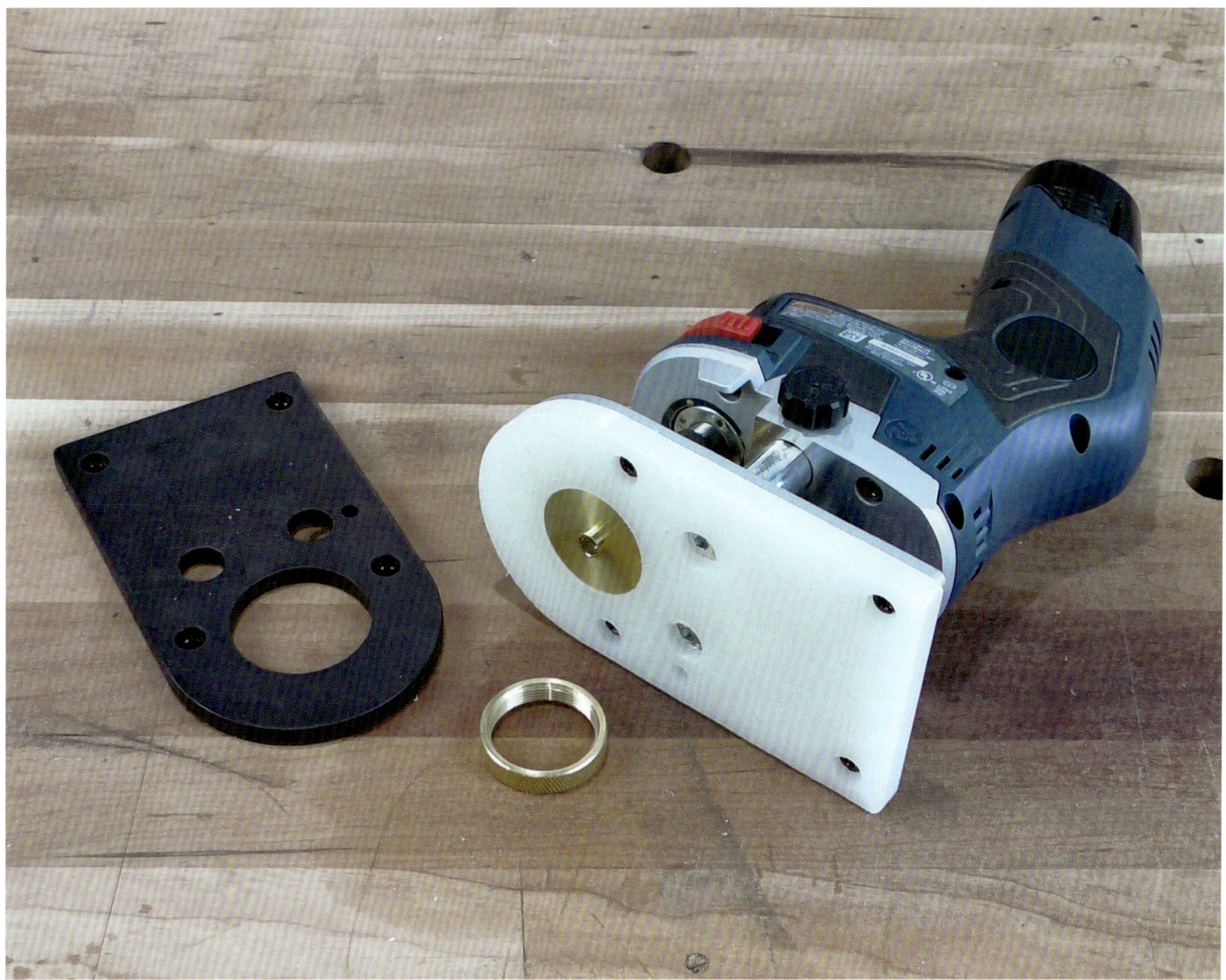

Nylons and polyethylenes are well suited for parts that need to slide and move easily.

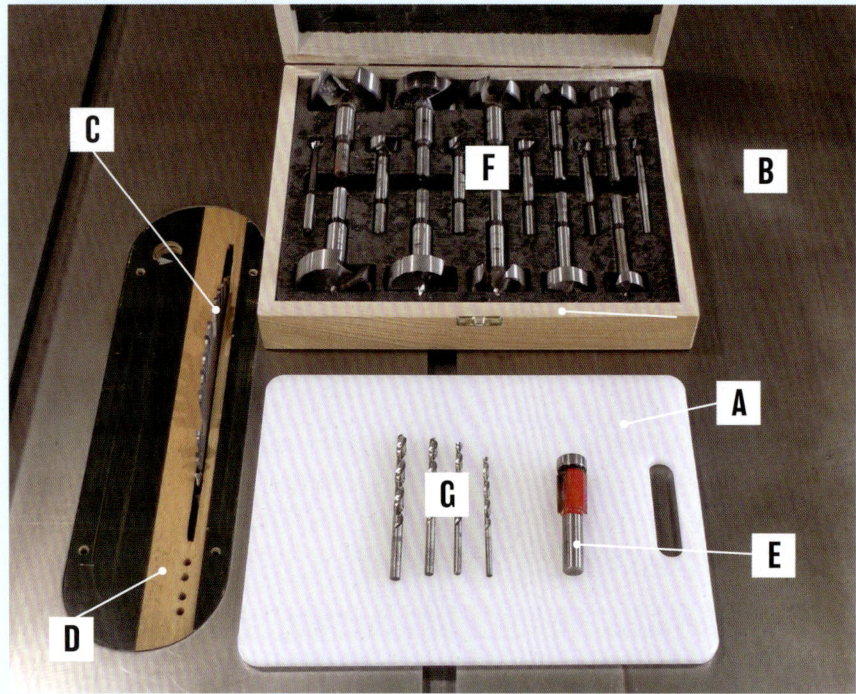

Plastics can be cut, routed, drilled, and tapped to create the parts needed.

Supplies:

- **A.** Nylon sheet, 0.375" (9.5mm) thick
- **B.** Table saw
- **C.** 10" (250mm) ATB or ATB-R combination blade, 50–60 tooth
- **D.** Zero-clearance throat plate insert
- **E.** Flush trim bit
- **F.** Forstner bits
- **G.** Drill bits
- **H.** Transfer punches or awl
- **I.** Mallet or hammer
- **J.** Bandsaw or coping saw
- **K.** Deburring tool or steel ruler

1. **Cut a piece of nylon to be slightly larger than you need.** I will be using my router's current base as a template, so I need to cut a 3 1/2" (90mm) x 6" (150mm) blank. A typical base like this must be at least 1/4" (6mm) thick to hold the bushing, but this router has some additional features along the bottom, so I need to make this replacement 3/8" (9.5mm) thick.

Alternative Nylon Source

You can buy a 3/8" (9.5mm) nylon sheet for this project from a local distributor or online. Kitchen cutting boards are also a great source of nylon in thicknesses from about 1/8"–1/2" (3–12mm), which is what I am using for my router base. I bought a new cutting board for the kitchen and used the old one for this project. The router base will not be hurt by a few knife marks.

An 11" (280mm) wide x 14" (350mm) long x 1/2" (12mm) thick cutting board was far less expensive than buying a similar-sized sheet of nylon stock. It did require an extra cut or two to remove the handle and juice groove, and you can't specify the exact size, but the cost is hard to beat.

With a bit of creativity, you may find alternative sources for your plastic supplies.

2. **Use the base plate as a template.** Remove the base plate from your router and secure it to the nylon blank using double-face tape. In addition to the guide bushing opening, this base requires several holes to be drilled. Mark through the base plate and onto the nylon. I use a set of transfer punches, but an awl can be used if you are careful to mark the center of each hole. Rap the transfer punches or awl to leave a physical mark or divot for each hole. Carefully mark the throat opening by scribing the circle with an awl; you can measure and mark the exact center later.

3. **Rough cut the nylon to shape using the bandsaw or a coping saw.** The soft nylon cuts very easily and the band saw blade does not heat up much as it passes through the cut; however, the flat back of the blade rubbing behind a tight turn could melt it. If any turns are too tight, just cut the waste by sections to get close to the base. This is just to remove the waste before flush trimming, so be careful not to cut into the router's base.

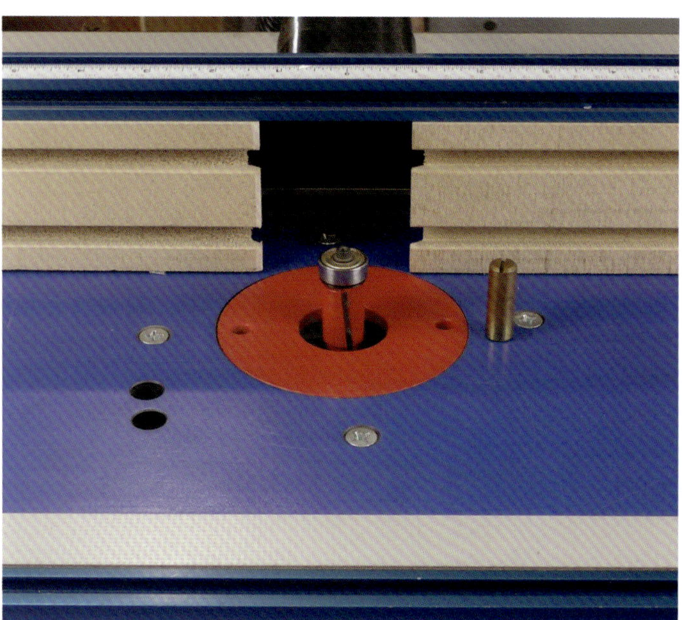

4. **Set up a flush trim bit in your router table.** Cut the nylon blank to size and shape using the original base as the template. Brace your part on a start pin before turning it into the router bit. The start pin provides a lever that helps prevent the bit from grabbing the part before the bearing reaches the template. A start pin is a simple thing that makes a big difference.

5. **Set the bit RPM as low as practical and keep the part moving as you trim.** If you need to move or rotate the part, pull it away from the bit while moving to prevent tool marks. You can tell if you are cutting at the right feed speed and RPM if the plastic is being cut into uniform flakes or curls. Dust means the RPM is too high or the part is not being fed across the bit fast enough.

6. **Separate the nylon blank from the router base once it is trimmed to size and shape.** Clean off the tape and move to the drill press. The guide bushings need a specific-sized counterbore hole. It is not hard to make if you follow the steps in order. Drill the counterbore first. It needs to be 1-3/8" (35mm) in diameter and 1/8" (3mm) deep.

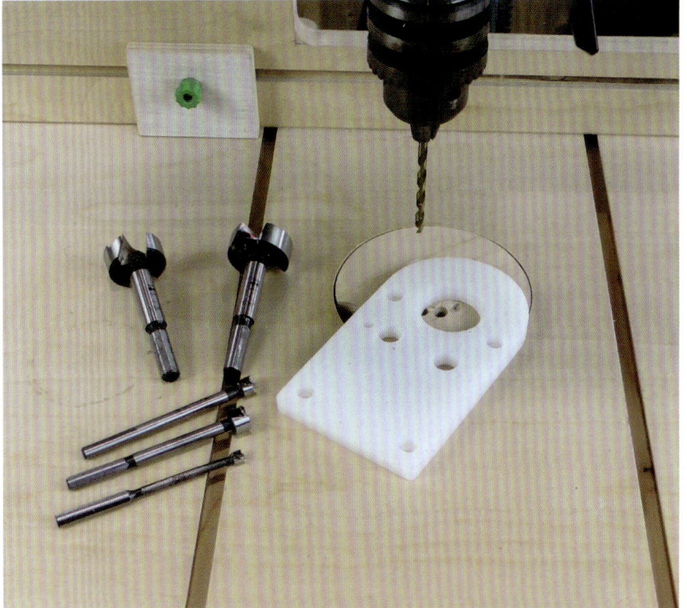

7. **Continue drilling the counterbore.** In the soft nylon, the Forstner bit may cut aggressively, so you can clamp the part in place if needed. Drill the hole to the 1/8" (3mm) depth and leave the part in place. The Forstner bit will leave a center point in the 1-3/8" (35mm) hole. Use this to guide the 1" (25mm) diameter Forstner bit to drill the throat opening through the nylon base. This leaves you with the proper size and shape hole to accept a standard guide bushing. The rest is just drilling the various counterbores and holes needed for mounting the base. Copy the size and depths of these holes from your factory base to get the best results.

8. **Ease all the edges of the router base.** Sharp tools create clean, sharp edges. The nylon is soft, but the crisp edges will be uncomfortable to hold and can catch in use. These edges can be sanded smooth or lightly scraped to break the sharp corners. You can use a deburring tool or even a steel ruler to do this. (See "Softening Edges by Hand" on page 81.) This is something you will find yourself doing regularly when working with plastics.

Upgrading Drill Bits

A general-purpose bit needs to be able to perform well in variety of materials.

Flattening the bevel angle behind the drilling edge is an easy way to improve drilling results in plastic.

Standard twist drill bits can create clean holes in plastics using the right techniques. But you can also easily reshape the cutting edge to produce consistently great results in all plastic types. Hard plastics like acrylic need to be well supported where the bit exits to avoid chipping and breakage. The bigger the bit diameter, the more care needs to be taken to control the drilling process and the exit point of through holes.

Standard bits sometimes "self-feed," especially in soft plastics; the tip of the bit can actually pull the bit into the material without being pushed. This can cause drilling deeper than intended for blind holes or breakage as the bit exits the plastic. Self-feeding can even lift the part into the drill if it is not secured to the bench or drill press. Self-feeding happens because the clearance bevel behind the cutting edge lets the bit pull itself into the cut as it turns.

Regrind the tip of a bit to avoid self-feeding in plastics. Look closely at the cutting edge of the bit. Note the angled face behind the cutting edge. The bit shown is for general purpose use; the factory angle is set to allow the bit to advance in a variety of materials. Grind this face to a shallower angle and it will resist self-feeding. The shallow bevel face will rub on the uncut plastic at the bottom of the hole, limiting how deep the bit can cut as it turns.

Use a grinding wheel when working with larger diameter bits and a hand file or rotary tool with smaller bits. Test-drill on some scrap plastic before and after grinding to get a feel for the best angle to use. Grind both tips to the same angle as closely as possible. It is not hard to regrind the tips, and with a bit of practice, you can get good results every time. It is still wise to back up the hole when drilling through any plastics, but this new grind will help you control the feed and greatly reduce chipping around the entry and exit of your holes.

Customize the bit for drilling plastics with just a few minutes of work.

3.2

ROUTER TABLE BIT GUARD

Plastics are invaluable as a source of protective covers over moving parts like gears and linkages. Clear plastics are useful where it is important to see the work area, such as with this router table bit guard. It is made of polycarbonate, which is usually clear and highly impact resistant. It is easy to work and even form without special tools.

This bit guard can be made using the drill press and band saw, but it lends itself quite well to being cut on a CNC machine and that is the method I use here. Any clean and sharp router bit will cut polycarbonate effectively, so you can use what you have on hand. The down shear spiral bit being used here cuts well in a wide variety of materials but is especially well suited to softer plastics like polycarbonate. The down shear cut also helps hold thin, flexible parts like this polycarbonate down on the table as it works. The spiral curve on the cutting edge slices the waste like a knife rather than chopping like a chisel. This makes for cleaner edges and lowers the risk of fracture in more brittle materials like acrylic.

The bit guard presented here was designed to fit my Kreg router table. You may need to alter your drawing to suit the application you have.

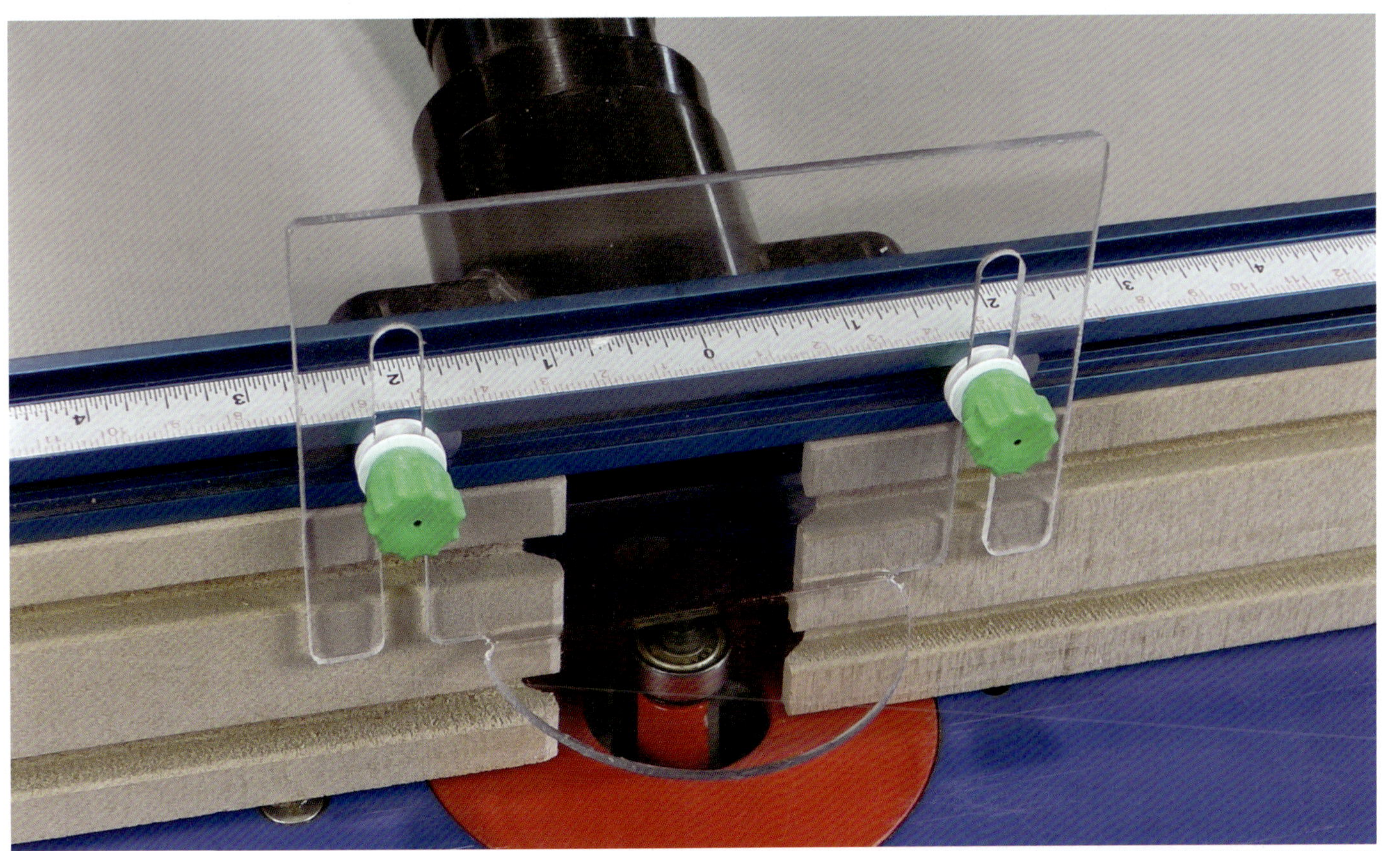

Whether you bought or built your router table, you can make a bit guard that works to keep your fingers safe.

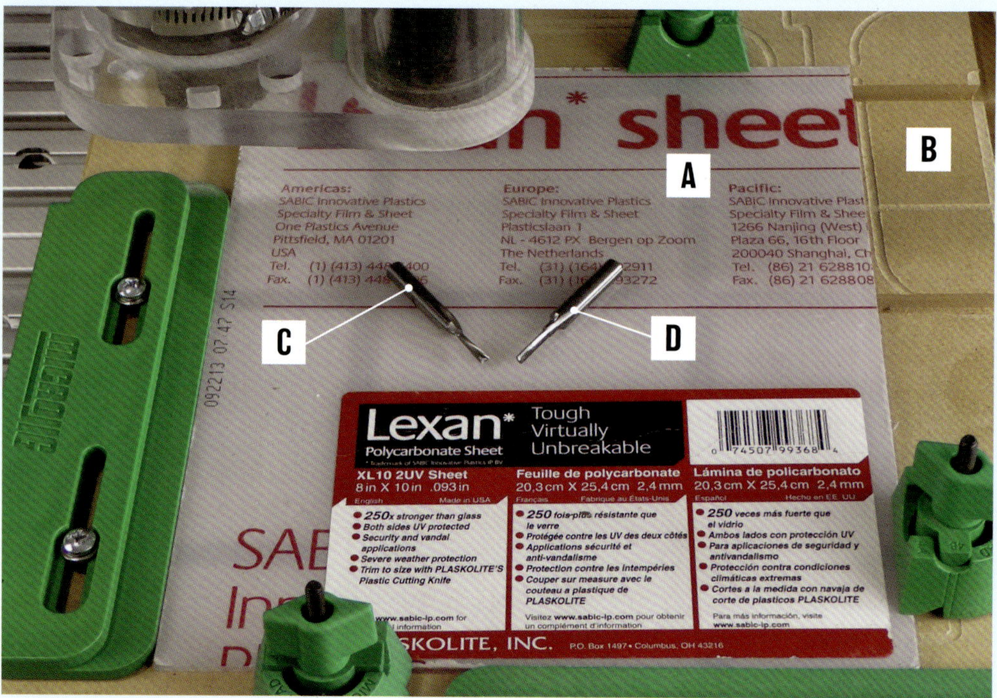

A CNC machine can cut plastics efficiently and eliminates the need for templates, jigs, and other woodworking machines.

Supplies:

- A. Polycarbonate sheet, 0.093" (2–3mm) thick
- B. CNC machine
- C. 1/8" (3mm) down shear spiral router bit
- D. 1/8" (3mm) straight router bit (optional)
- E. Deburring tool or steel ruler

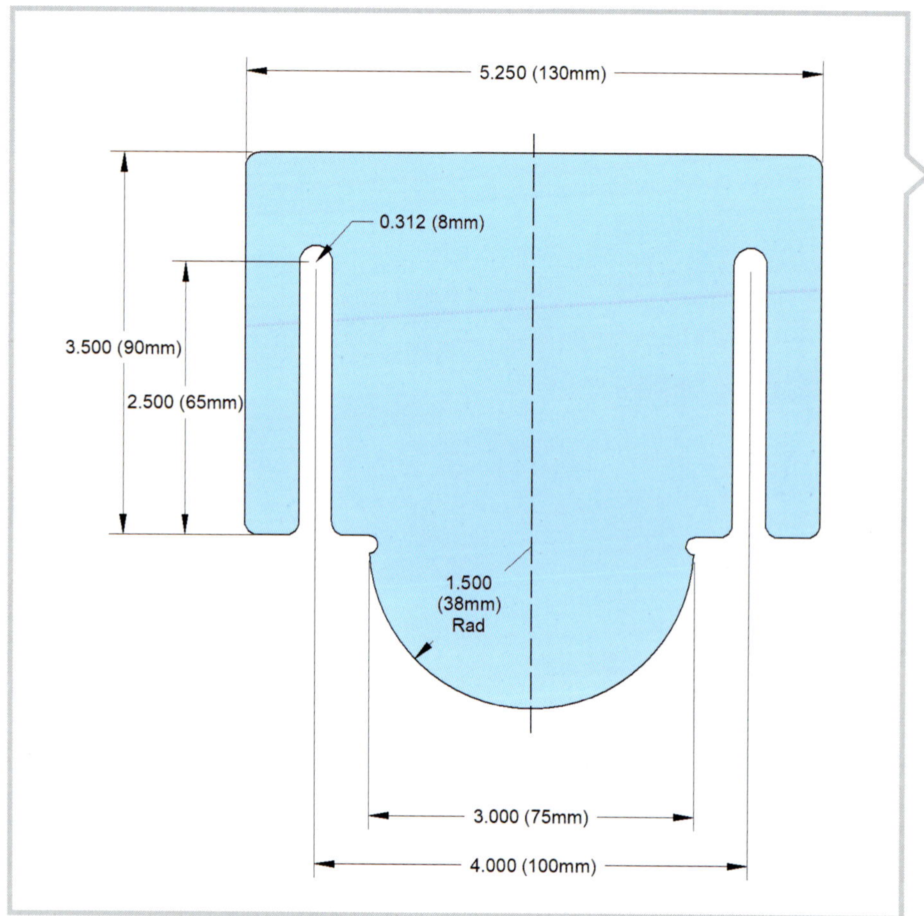

1. **Create the drawing with your CAD/CAM software.** Note that the slots are meant for 1/4-20 (M6 x 1mm) hardware, so they are cut at 5/16" (8mm) wide to allow for moving easily over the bolt threads. There is also a pair of small notches in the final part where the circular guard portion begins. This will mark the bend line later. Using the CNC makes adding and changing these details easy.

Bits, Feeds, and Speeds for Plastics

The chips being cut from your plastics can tell you if your feed and speed (inches per minute and RPM) settings are correct. The goal is to have clean, uniform flakes flying out of the cut line. Beads of melted plastic in and along the kerf is an obvious sign of excessive heat. The heat is from the friction of the cutting edge against the stock. Moving the bit too slow causes unwanted heat as does spinning the bit too fast. Just as with wood, you want to create chips and flakes, not dust.

The CNC machine allows you to accurately program a series of test cuts to find the best settings for the work to be done. Program a cut using your best guess at the proper RPM and feed rate. If you see evidence of melting, you can raise the feed rate or lower the RPM. Doing either, or even both, will reduce the rubbing of the cutter on any given section of the plastic, reducing the heat and improving the cut. As you test different bit settings with different plastics, you will develop a feel for what works best.

The CNC allows for testing cut quality at known RPM and feed rates in whatever materials you are using.

The chips inside the cut closest to the camera are clearly smaller and less well formed than with other tests.

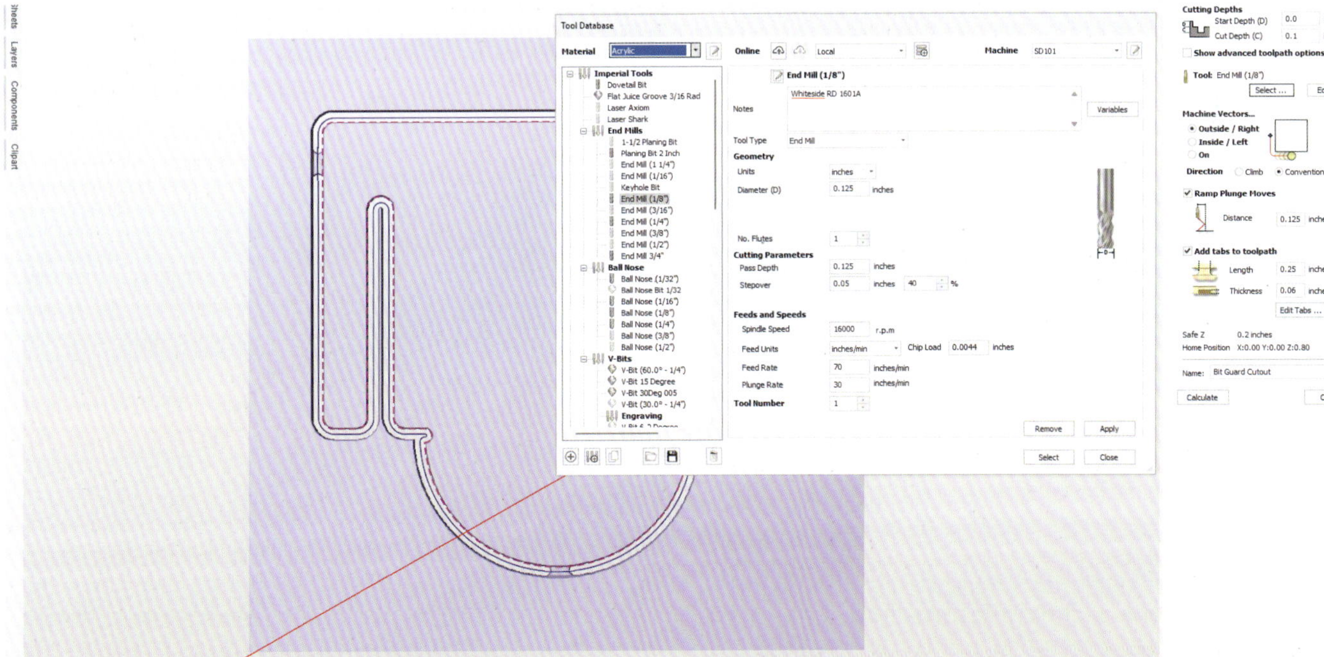

2. **Secure the stock onto the bed of your CNC machine.** This sheet came with the plastic film protective layer; for this project, leave it in place. For projects made up of small parts or those that have a lot of fine details, it can be better to remove the film before cutting to minimize time spent peeling small sections after the cutting is complete. Run the program to cut out the parts.

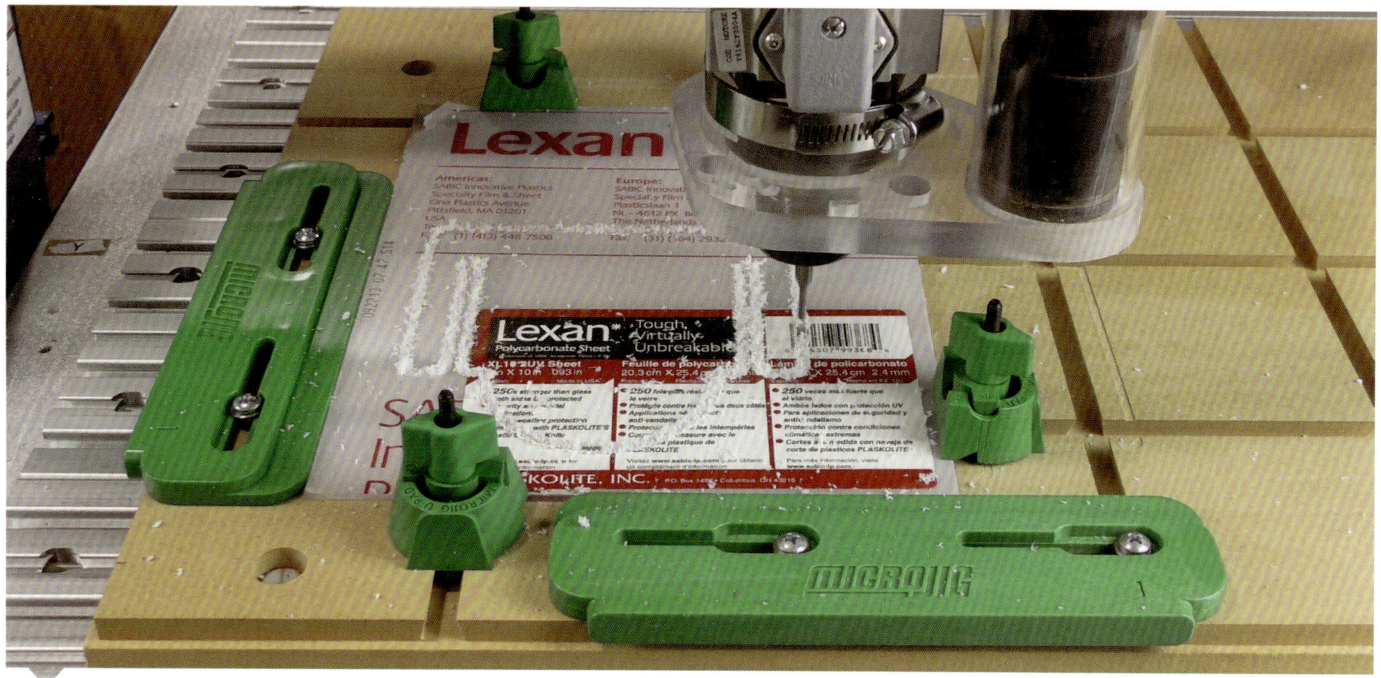

3. **Check the CNC as it runs.** Tabs were used here to hold the part to the blank, but this is a case where double-face tape can be used. At this point, you can tell if your cut settings are correct. You should see uniform flakes of plastic left by the bit. Fine dust or balls of melted plastic mean your feed rate is too slow, your RPM is too high, or both. Dust means extra friction heat—and as ever, heat is to be avoided (see the sidebar on page 61).

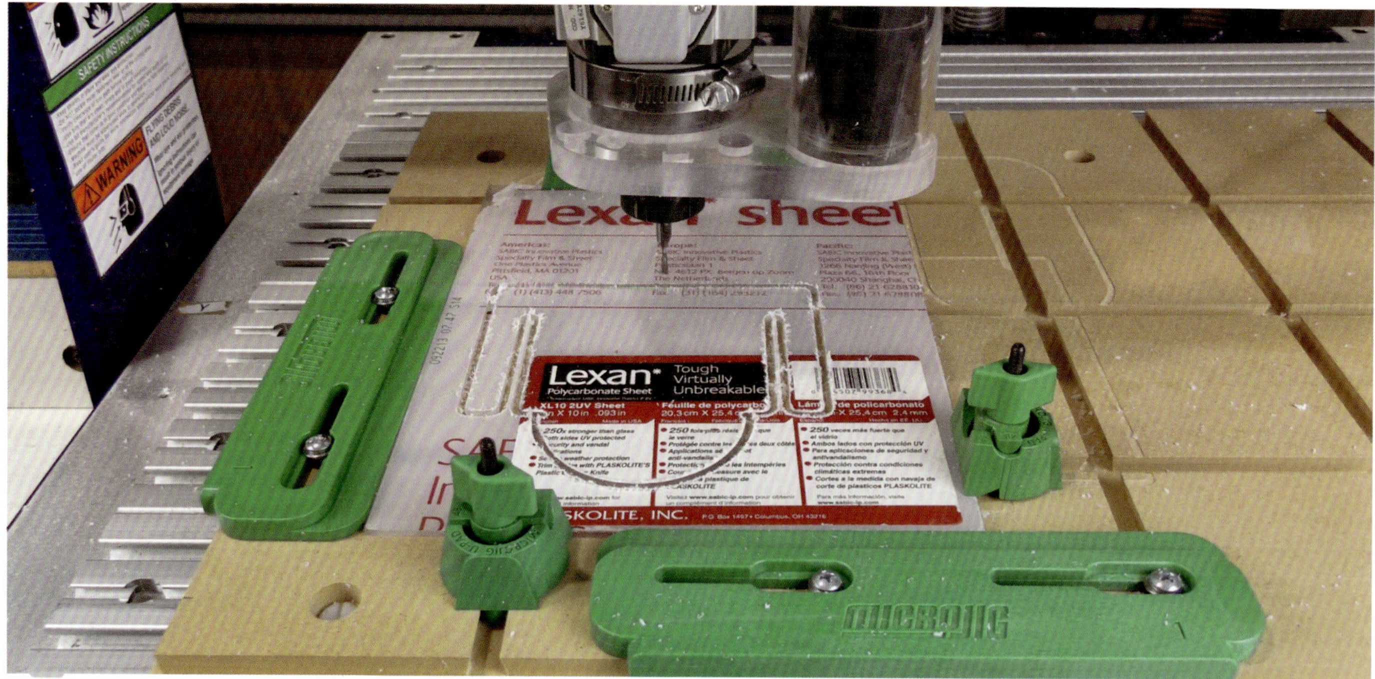

4. **Remove the part from the machine.** Cut the tabs or peel the double-face tape off to separate the part from the waste. The edges should be relatively clean but may be sharp if the bit cut cleanly. Ease the edges using a deburring tool or your trusty steel ruler. The part is ready for bending, which will be done in Chapter 6.1. Note the small indentations at the base of the round guard part. These were cut to mark the proper bend line. This is one of the details that CNC machines make quick and accurate, and it is a lot less work than cutting out parts from a printed template.

3.3 LIGHTED SIGN GRAPHIC

Transparent plastics can be made to look like neon signs. Letters or images are carved into the body, the carvings tend to glow when the edges of the plastic are illuminated. This can work for clear or colored acrylics. A sign of this type can be made using many of the same techniques and tools you are familiar with from your woodworking. This sign project is an excellent chance to compare techniques side by side. The shape will be made with the bandsaw and router table, the text on the CNC, and the graphic with a hand router.

Edge lighting—engraved acrylic creates a neon effect that really shines at night.

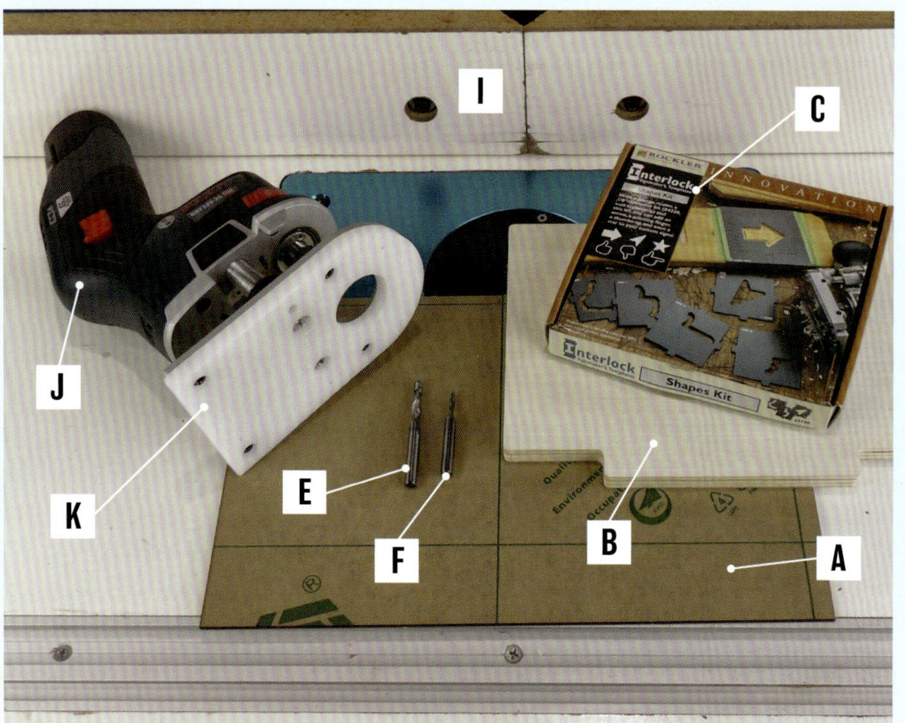

This project uses different tools and methods for milling and engraving the acrylic sheet.

Supplies:

- **A.** Acrylic sheet, 0.125" (3mm) thick
- **B.** Plywood template, 1/2" (12mm) thick
- **C.** Router stencil set
- **D.** Inlay guide bushing (here, included in stencil set)
- **E.** 1/8" (3mm) router bit
- **F.** Small-diameter flush trim router bit
- **G.** CNC machine (optional)
- **H.** Bandsaw
- **I.** Router table
- **J.** Handheld router
- **K.** Nylon router base from Chapter 3.1

1. **Copy the template drawing onto the plywood.** Cut and sand it to shape as you would any plywood template. Sand all edges smooth—any flaws in the template will be transferred to the acrylic parts when flush trimming. Stick the template onto the acrylic sheet and use the bandsaw to rough cut the acrylic to the traced line. To prevent cracking, keep the acrylic tight to the bandsaw table. Cut only in straight lines; the rear of the bandsaw blade will melt any plastic edges it rubs against. The flush trim bit will remove the excess and create the rounded corners, so they do not need to be formed here.

2. **Using the flush trim bit in your router table, trim the acrylic to the shape of the template.** Use a start pin to control the part as the cut starts. The start pin prevents the bit from grabbing the stock, which leads to chipping or breaking the acrylic. Work steadily around the template and avoid pausing in any one spot. Pull the part away from the bit when you need to stop or shift your grip. Rubbing causes friction and friction creates heat. The cut edge should be clean, and the chips should be uniform in shape and size as you cut. If you see melting on the edges or dust instead of chips, turn the RPM down and keep the part moving as you cut. Once it is cut to final shape, separate the template from the acrylic sheet carefully. Inspect the edges to ensure that there are no cracks or flaws that need to be fixed.

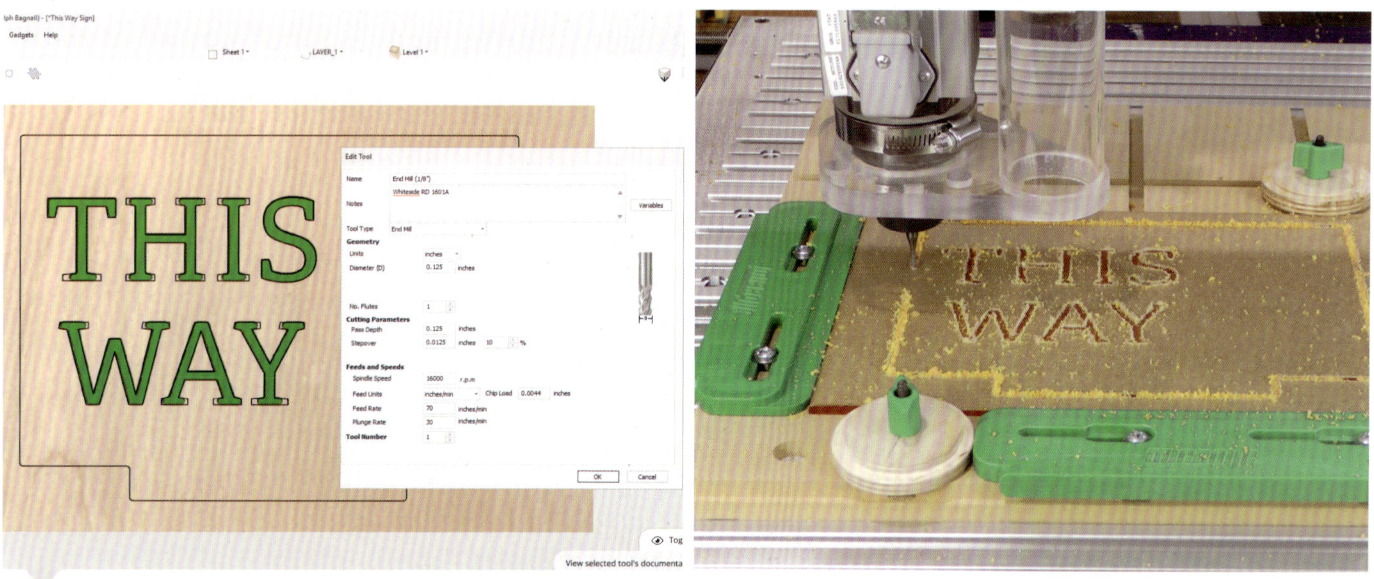

3. **Carve the text into the acrylic using your CNC machine.** Program the text for the sign in your CAD/CAM software. The example shown is set up to carve using a 1/8" (3mm) bit cutting about halfway through the material, so 0.062" (1.5mm) deep. Mount the 1/8" (3mm) bit into the CNC machine; you will use the same bit in the hand router. Using the same bit will ensure the cuts are similar. Leave the paper film on the acrylic sheet for this cutting. As before, test cuts can be made in scrap samples of the sheet to verify the feed and speed for the bit. In this case, the bit was turning at 12,000 RPM with a cut speed of 70 inches per minute. If you do not have a CNC, the lettering can be cut using templates following the method in steps 4 and 5.

4. **Set the router stencil on the acrylic to hand cut the graphic.** My stencil set uses a frame with various inserts, each of which cuts a section of the image. I am using the pointing hand set here. Fit the router with the inlay guide bushing. My trim router is fitted with the nylon guide bushing base from Chapter 3.1. This router is lightweight and easier to control than a larger router when following this small, complex template. Set the cut depth of the bit to match the text carving just completed. Set the barrel of the guide bushing into the groove in the template part and mill away all the plastic the bit can reach. Try to keep the bit moving without pause to avoid heat. Lift the router off the stencil if you need to pause or check your work.

5. **Work through the stencils until the graphic is fully cut.** This pointing hand required three parts. It is a good idea to practice this stencil cutting on scrap plastic until you get used to the technique, especially for small and irregular shapes. The acrylic sign is ready to be edge polished (Chapter 4) and set on a lighted base.

3.4 NAPKIN HOLDER PARTS

This mid-century modern napkin holder combines plywood and plastic in a way that is a perfect example of why your woodshop may need to be able to cut and thermoform plastic sheet. The parts need to be machined, edge polished, thermoformed, and mechanically fastened. The process starts here by milling the wood and plastic parts using the CNC machine. As shown in Chapter 3.3, parts like this can always be made using templates and more traditional machines.

A napkin holder is an excellent example of woodworking augmented with worked plastic parts.

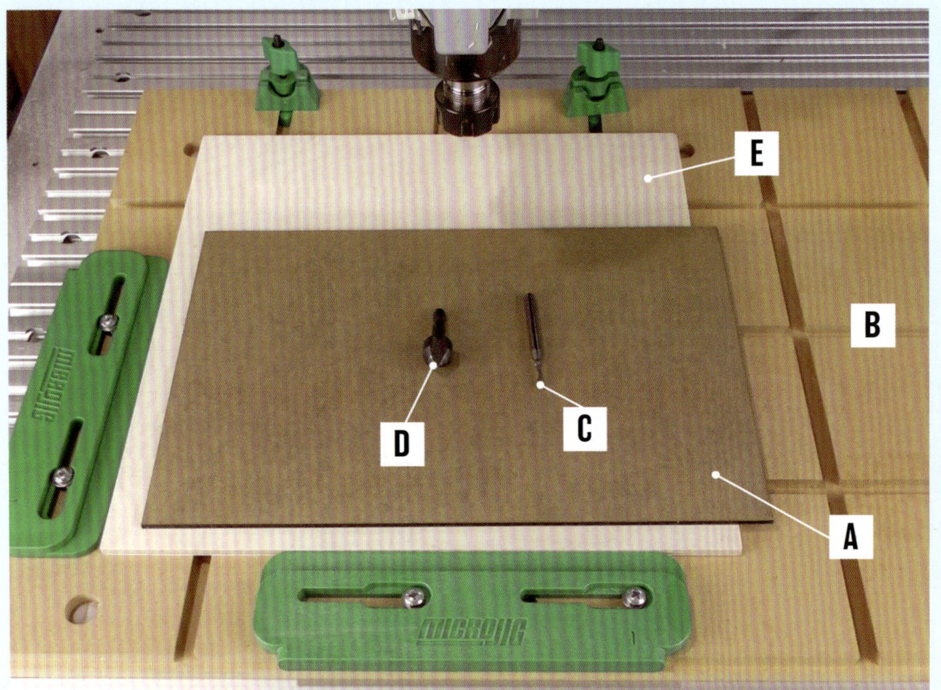

The plastic and wood parts use the same bits and procedures, simplifying the cutting on the CNC or by hand.

Supplies:

- **A.** Colored acrylic sheet, 0.125" (3mm) thick
- **B.** CNC machine
- **C.** 1/8" (3mm) router bit
- **D.** Countersink
- **E.** Baltic birch plywood, 12" (300mm) wide x 12" (300mm) long x 1/4" (6mm) thick
- **F.** Plywood cutting template (optional)

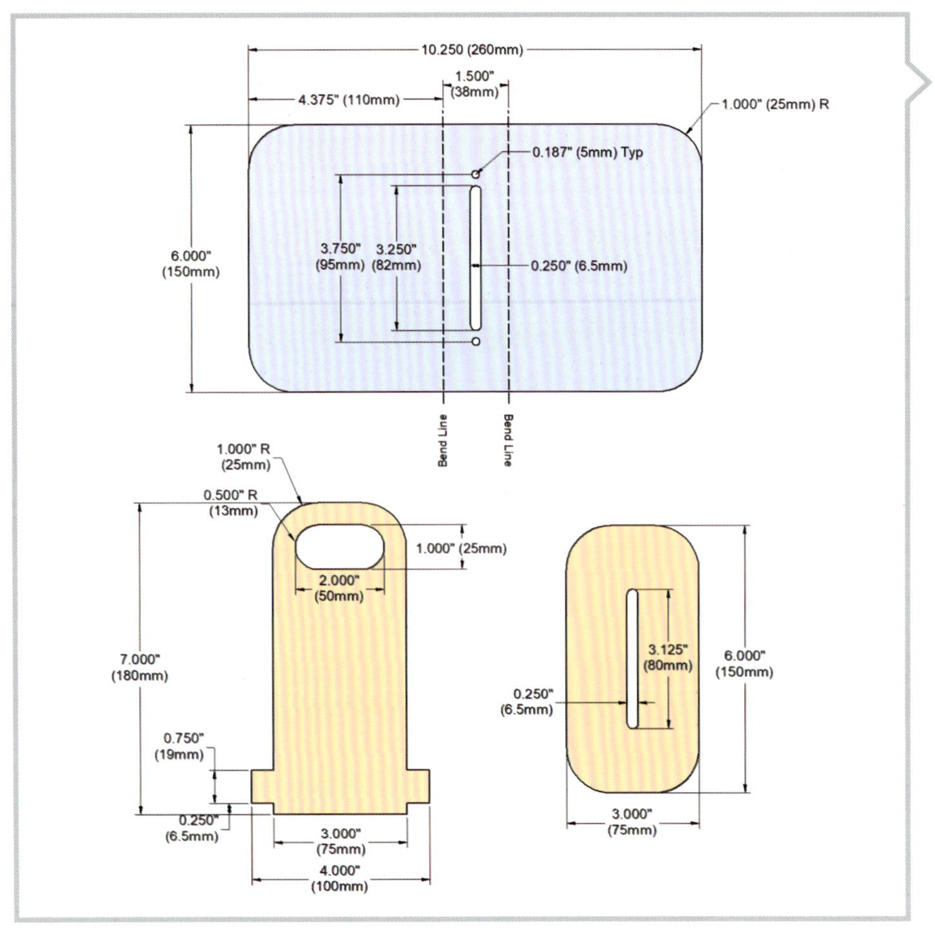

1. Program the CAD/CAM software for the CNC machine. You will be creating the napkin holder blank in the acrylic and the stand parts in plywood. Both can be cut out using the same 1/8" (3mm) straight bit. The dimensions shown are for 5" (125mm) or 6" (150mm) square napkins. You can adjust the design if you have a different size. Optionally, a plywood template can be created for shaping the plastic using saws and the router table (see Chapter 3.3). The rectangular shape with well-rounded corners features a slot in the center for the stand as well as two small countersunk holes for screws.

2. **Mill the acrylic part using the router bit.** Leave the protective film in place for milling. The cut testing done in Chapter 3.1 should give you a good idea of the feeds and speeds needed. Countersink the two mounting holes to accept a small screw head. These need to be done now, as they will be on the inside of the bent plastic holder. A multi-flute countersink works best with plastic, but a single flute countersink works fine too. Apply light pressure as you work, letting the tool scrape the hole sides to form a counterbore to fit #4 brass screws.

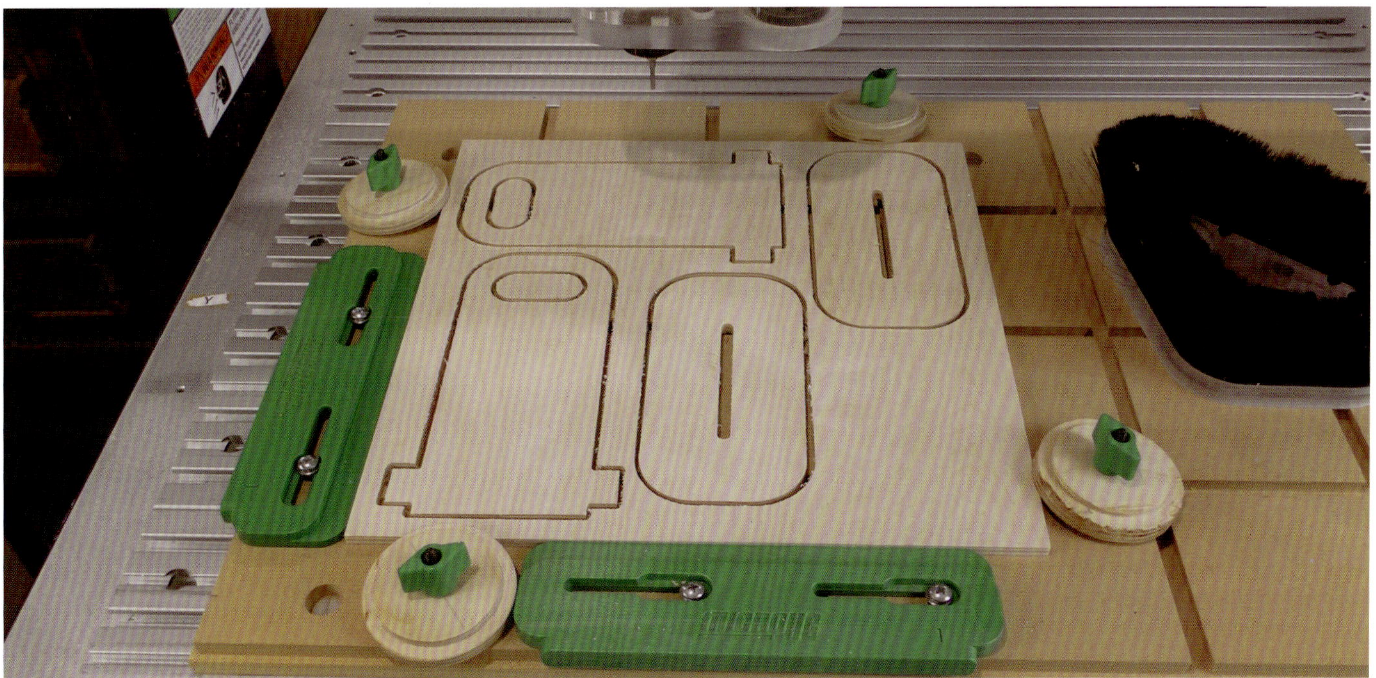

3. **Cut the plywood parts while the CNC is set up.** The same bits that cut your typical woodworking will generally work with most plastics. Cut the wood parts from the waste then clean and sand the edges ready for finishing. The edges of the plastic parts will be fully visible, so they need to be highly polished. It is much easier to work the edges while the part is still flat and has the cover film protecting it, so this will be done in Chapter 4.2 before bending in Chapter 6.4 and decorating in Chapter 5.2.

3.5

LASER-ENGRAVED SIGN

Most types of lasers can generally mark plastics to some degree, but real engraving and cutting through clear or translucent plastics typically requires a CO2 laser. These tend to be more expensive than the common diode lasers that are seen across online retailers. Laser cutting and engraving plastics are really beyond the scope of this book, but I wanted to include a look at how parts like this little sign can be marked without needing major new equipment. It does assume some sort of diode laser engraver in the shop.

Lasers are now common in woodshops and—within limits—can be used for engraving and cutting plastics.

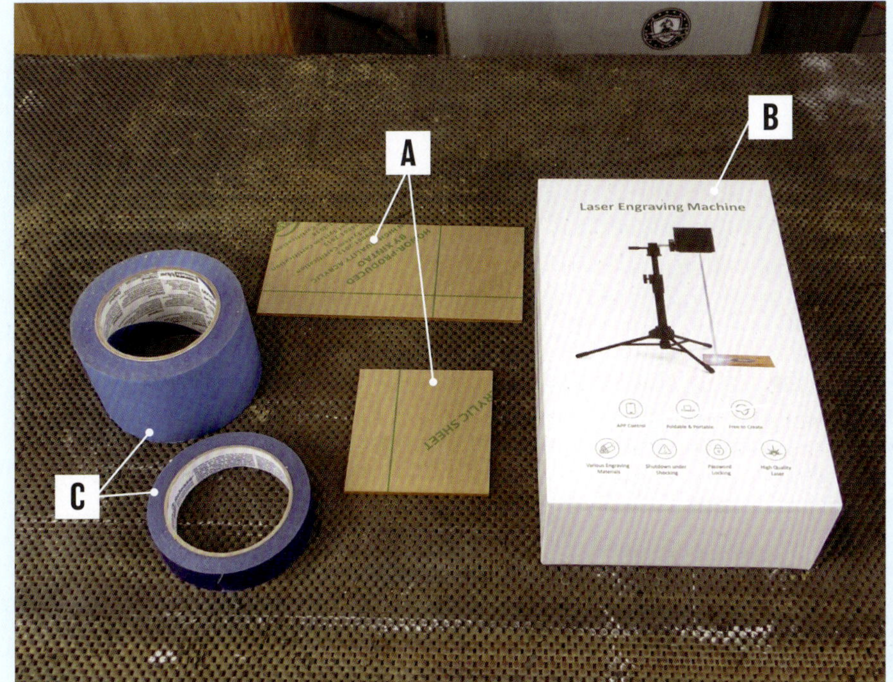

This inexpensive laser can't cut plastic but can mark plastics if used correctly.

Supplies:

- **A.** Clear/translucent plastic sheet
- **B.** Diode laser
- **C.** Painter's tape (optional)

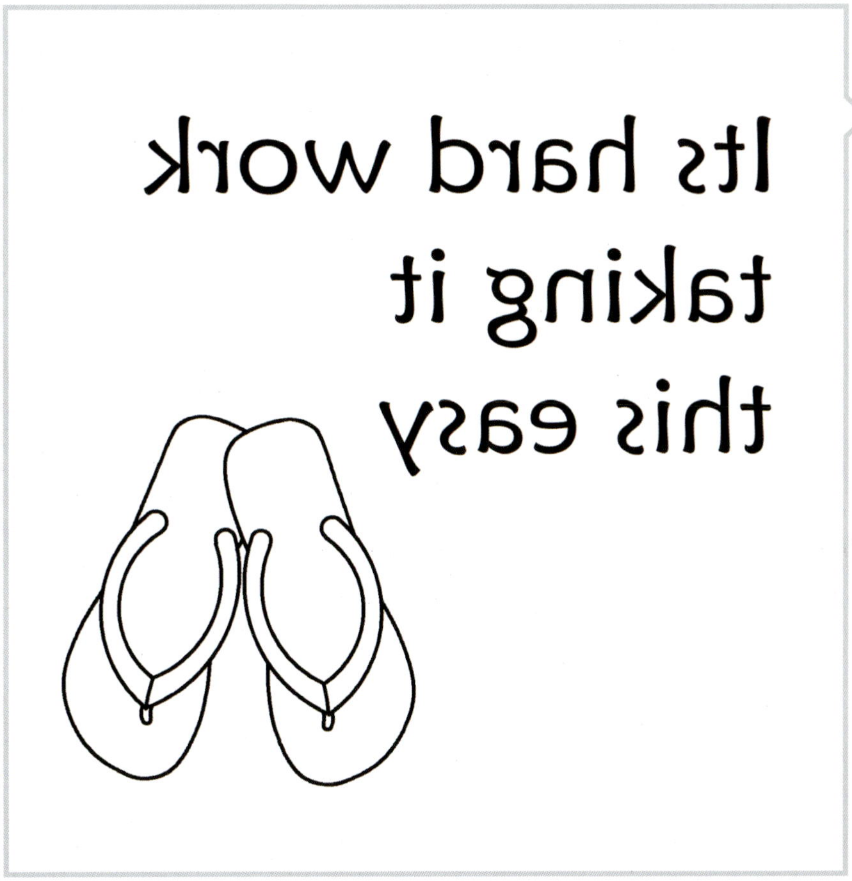

1. **Create the artwork to be engraved.** I use a phone app to turn images into engravings. Commercial CAD/CAM programs like LightBurn are designed for more complex programming. The artwork here was created in my CAD program and saved as a .JPG. I found that for edge lighting, engraving the back of the part worked better, so I mirrored the drawing. Cut the plastic to size and shape. Prepare the edges before engraving (see Chapter 4). This sign will be edge lit, which requires the edges to be polished clear. To keep the surface free from scratches, leave the paper film on the plastic or use painter's tape.

Engraving Hacks

Lasers use light to cut and engrave, so except for CO2 lasers, they tend not to work well on clear items like glass and plastic. My research for this book turned up many articles online that recommend painting the plastic surface with black tempera or milk paint. The laser will burn off the paint, melting into the plastic underneath as it does. This works well for the engraving, but I found that washing off the paint led to scratches no matter how carefully I worked. Minor scratches often would not be an issue, but for this sort of edge-lit sign, every scratch shows up no matter how small.

As a test, I tried leaving the paper protective film on the plastic and lasering onto that instead of paint. A few tests showed that setting my laser to the correct power cut through the paper and deep enough into the plastic to work as I wanted. If your plastic comes with the clear film, remove that and apply a layer of painter's tape to cover the area being engraved.

2. **Align the plastic under the laser.** This unit has a stationary head with mirrors that aim the laser. I created a target sheet that helps to locate the image to be engraved. Other systems may have a head that travels over the stock to cut the image. This unit runs a low-power preview, which shows the area to be engraved before the program starts. Set the power of the laser to cut through the paper and into the plastic. I found that 75%–100% power left a very nice marking in the part, but note that the laser shown is a very low-power system, only meant for light marking. Lasers are constantly coming out with higher power options. Make test cuts using your laser system to get the results you want.

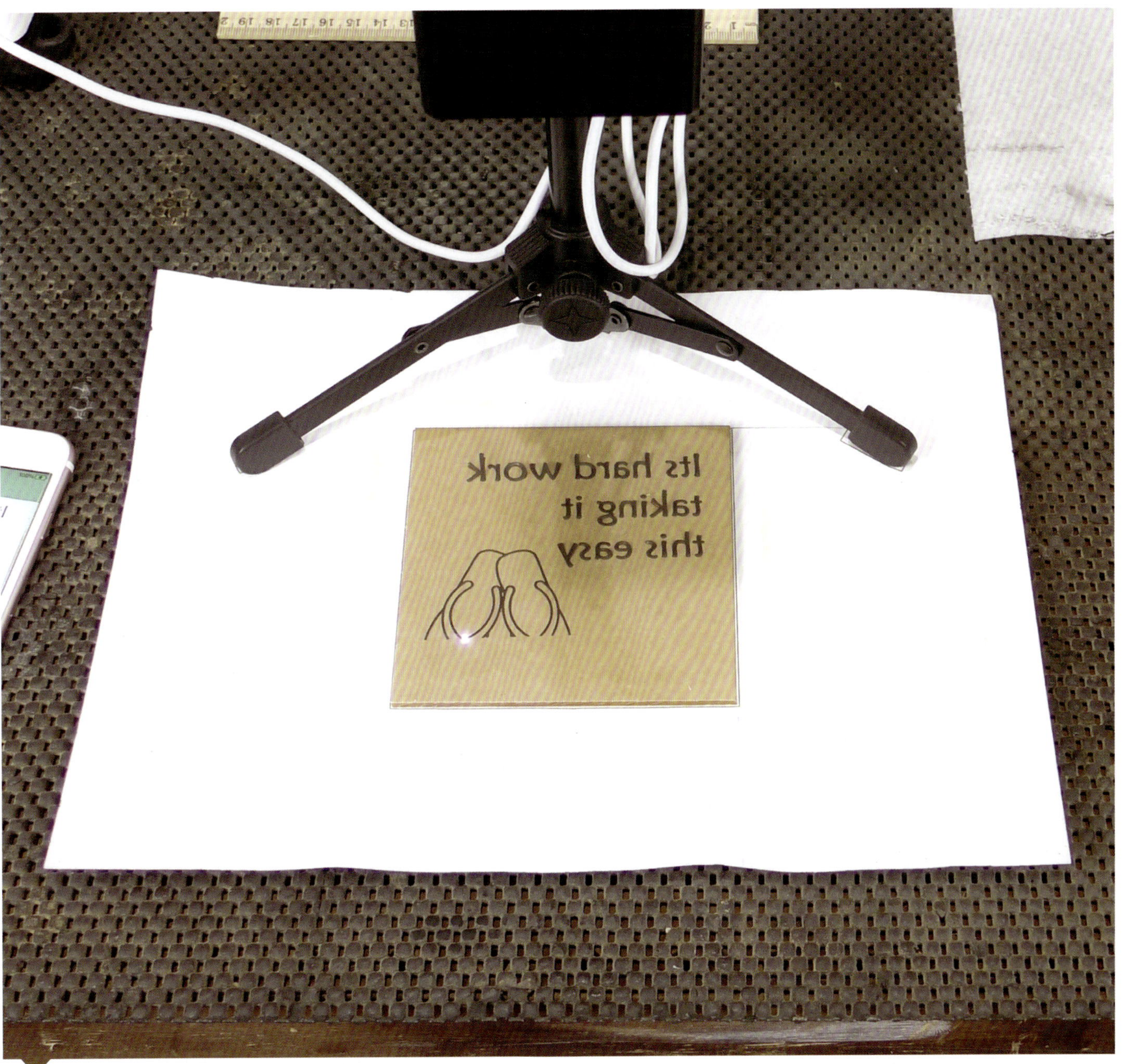

3. **Run the engraving program.** The machine shown passes side to side down the working area like an ink-jet printer. Larger machines use x- and y-axis drives to mark larger areas. This 4" (100mm) x 4" (100mm) image takes about 20 minutes and runs independently. Remember to provide good ventilation while laser engraving on any materials. Peel the paper layer off. The protective paper is designed to release easily, and painter's tape is low tack; even so, work carefully to avoid scratching the surface. Depending on your design, there may be many small bits to remove inside letters and graphics. You may need to gently wash the surface if there is any soot left behind from the burning. The plastic cleaner from Chapter 5.6 is designed for plastic and prevents static.

3.6
BUSHINGS FOR TURNING

Just about all plastics can be turned on the lathe. Over the years, I have made many stand-offs, adapters, knobs, and other items for projects. Many insert turning tools are now available with cutting edges designed specifically for acrylic and epoxy resin turning. These cone-shaped mandrels are being turned from nylon and can be worked with almost any turning tools.

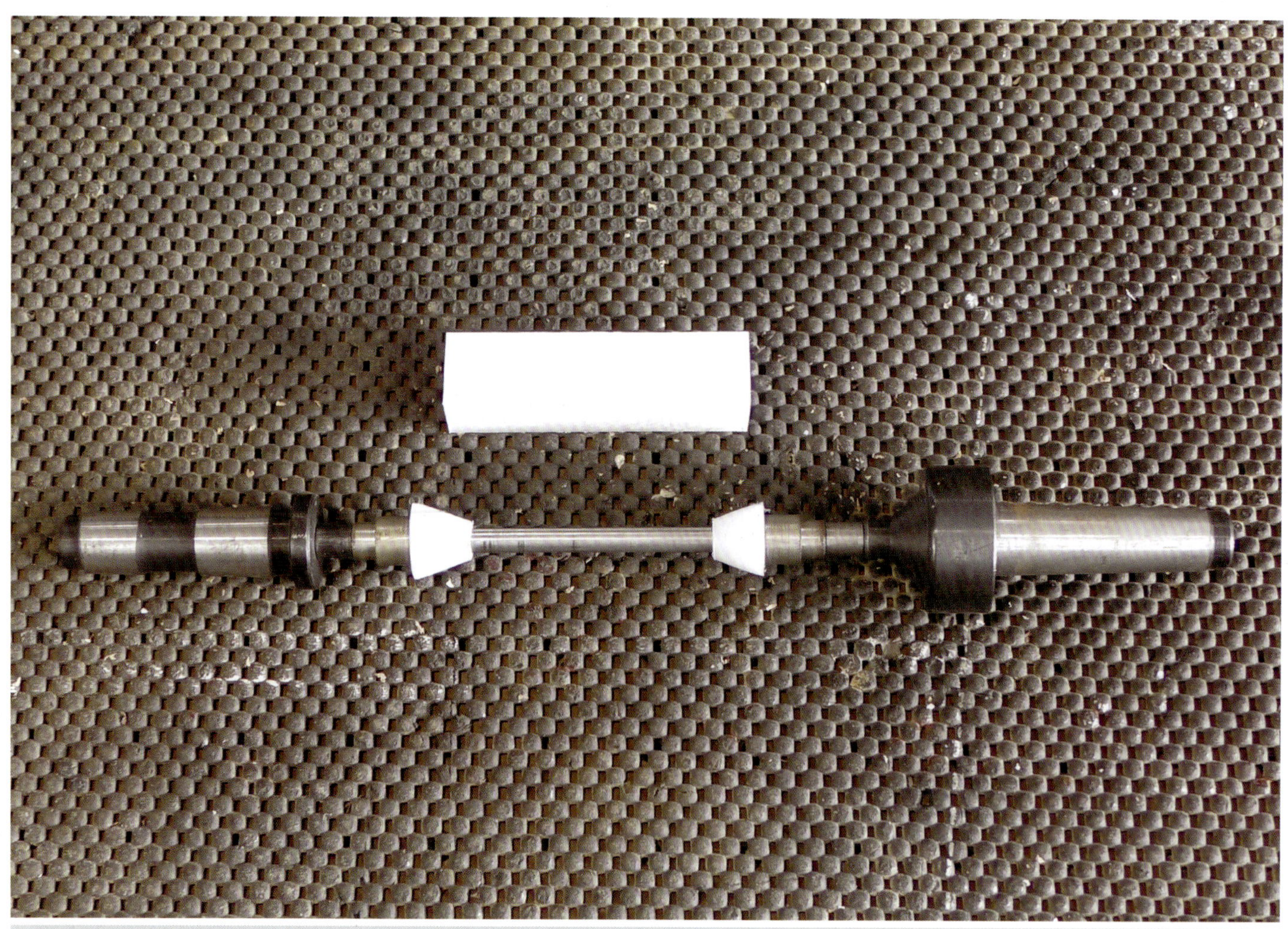

Conical bushings will fit pen turning projects with a range of tube sizes.

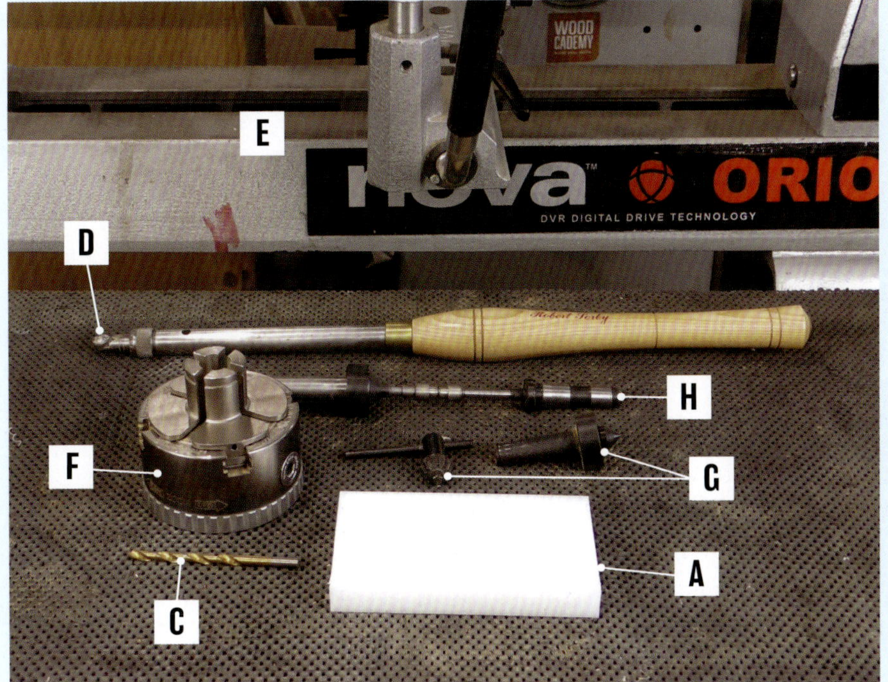

This project can be completed with just the basic turning tools if needed.

Supplies:

- A. Nylon sheet, 3/4" (19mm) thick
- B. Nylon rod, 3/4" (19mm) diameter (optional)
- C. 1/4" (6.4mm) drill bit
- D. Turning tools (rough, finish, and parting)
- E. Lathe
- F. Jaw chuck (optional)
- G. Drill chuck (optional)
- H. Pen turning mandrel
- I. Utility knife or fine-tooth hand saw

1. **Cut the nylon stock to size.** I used some of the leftover stock from Chapter 2.3, ripped to 3/4" (19mm) wide and crosscut to 3" (75mm) long. If you are using rod stock, you can simply cut it to 3" (75mm) long.

2. **Drill a hole through the center of the nylon blank to fit your mandrel.** The shaft on this one is 1/4" (6.4mm) but check yours. You can drill this on the drill press using the fence with a stop, or with a pen turning drill guide. The hole does not have to be perfectly centered because turning the stock will center it. I have clamped the blank into the jaw chuck for my lathe and have the bit mounted in a drill chuck. This setup lets me drill the part on the lathe, which can be very accurate and is one less tool that needs to be set up.

3. **Mount the blank on the pen mandrel and turn it to diameter.** I set the lathe to about 1,200 RPM and used my roughing tool to turn it to about 5/8" (16mm) diameter. Unlike turning wood, as the part becomes round, the shavings will turn into long thin ribbons rather than breaking into chips. These can wind around the part and mandrel pretty quickly. This is not dangerous, but you will need to clear them as you work.

4. **Shape the cone in the nylon.** Use a finishing tool as shown here or a skew chisel if that is what you have. Acrylics work better on the lathe with specialized tools, but the softer plastics can be formed with all the common turning tools. I formed two matching cones facing each other with a short thin section in between to make the parting easier.

5. **Cut the two cones most of the way off the waste using a parting tool.** Do not cut all the way through the plastic because the tool and rod can both be damaged if they come into contact. Cut them most of the way through, remove the nylon part from the mandrel, then cut the bushings off the waste with a utility knife or a fine-tooth hand saw.

6. **Use cone-shaped bushings to hold parts centered on your mandrel over any size hole within the range of the cone you make.** This is useful for holes you make that may be an odd size, and the cones can replace having to buy custom bushings to fit the various tube sizes of turning kits.

4

Chapter 4: Edge-Finishing Plastics

Many clear plastic parts you make will need to have some sort of edge-finishing done. This may be as simple as easing the sharp edges or as fancy as polishing them to transparency. This chapter will continue working on the projects started in previous chapters, with lessons on achieving the finish that each one needs.

4.1

SKYLINE WINDOW HANGER

Cut edges of parts usually need to be smoothed and cleaned up, especially with clear plastics. There are three methods for how to start depending on the edge quality needed. The initial steps are the same for most projects, and this skyline window hanger only needs the most basic treatment. Other projects in this book require more work, but they all start with the instructions that follow.

Sawn edges are fine inside a frame where they are never seen, but for this frameless artwork, they need to be more presentable.

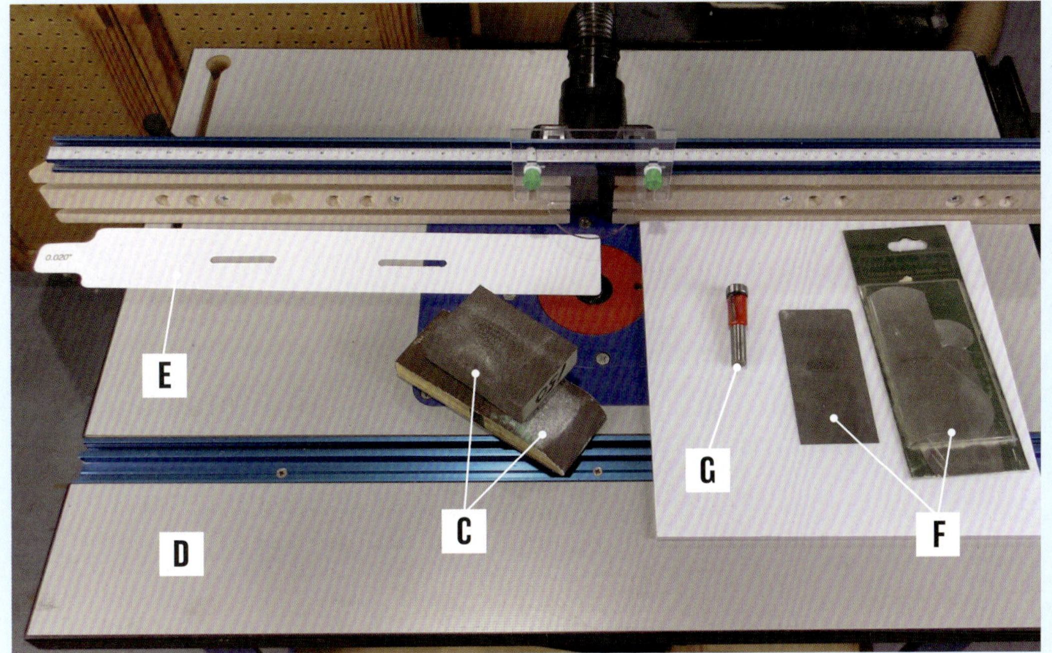

Virtually every shop has at least the basic tools needed to treat acrylic edges.

Supplies:

- **A.** Acrylic blank from Chapter 2.2
- **B.** Jointer
- **C.** Sanding block
- **D.** Router table (optional)
- **E.** Spacer shim from Chapter 1.2 (optional)
- **F.** Cabinet scraper or steel ruler (optional)
- **G.** Flush trim bit (optional)

1a. **Smooth the freshly cut edges before sanding or polishing to save time and avoid heat stress.** Edges that have been scored and snapped (see Chapter 2.1) or cut at the table saw can be smoothed using a jointer or router table. This process will remove some material, so that needs to be considered with the initial cutting to size. The jointer should have sharp blades and be set to a very shallow cut: 1/32" (1mm) or even less. Run straight edges across the jointer slowly to create a smooth edge. In many cases, this will be all the finishing needed.

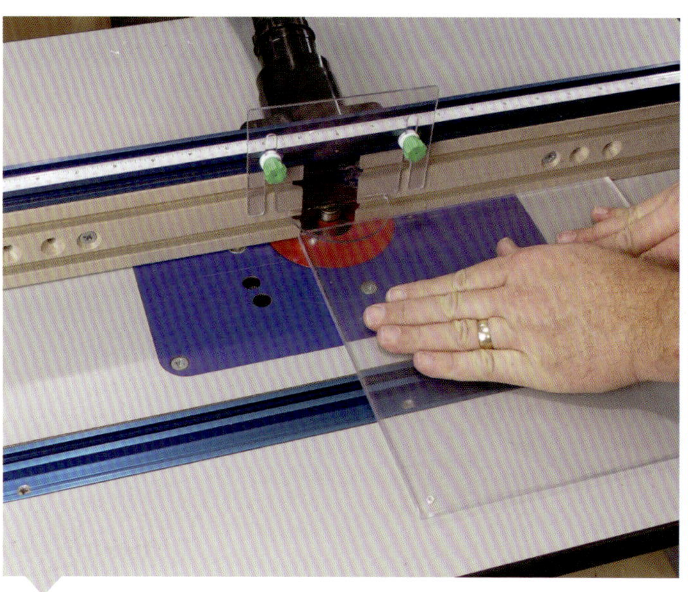
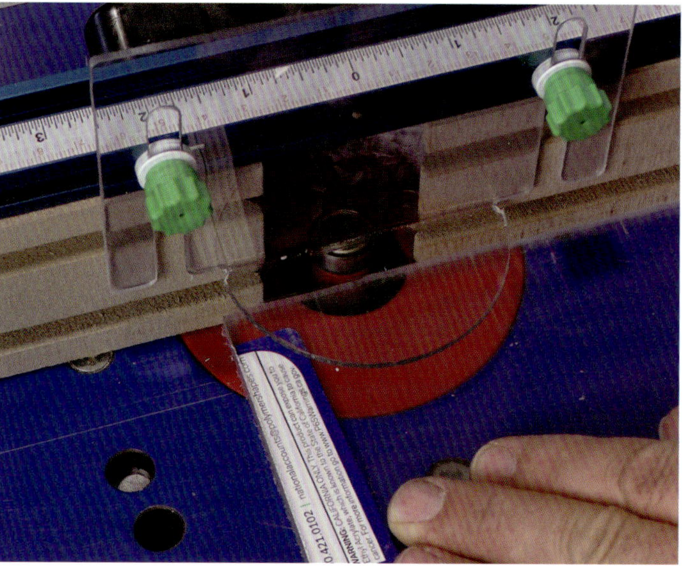

1b. **Use a router table with split fences in place of a jointer.** Shim the outfeed face for a 0.02" (0.5mm) cut. Set the fence so this outfeed is flush with the cutter. This setup will allow the router table to act as a jointer but with the stock on its side instead of on edge. Use the largest-diameter bit that is practical. The larger cutting circle makes a cleaner cut, and the larger bit dissipates heat better. Again, a slow feed rate will provide the smoothest cut.

1c. **Smooth the raw edges by hand in place of a jointer or router table.** This can be done with a cabinet scraper or even a simple steel ruler. Hold the tool across the plastic and push or pull it along the edge, leaning at about a 30-degree angle in the direction of the cut. The edges can be softened at this point as well. This level of finish would be perfectly fine in many cases, but these edges will be quite visible, so one more step is needed.

Softening Edges by Hand

When you cut plastics properly, there is some hazard that comes from the very clean square edges. Acrylic edges can be sharp enough to cut flesh and damage surfaces they contact, even other plastic parts. Sanding is one way of "breaking" these sharp edges and can be done with a sanding block. There are also a number of simple tools that make it easy to soften single parts and those that have odd shapes.

A deburring tool like the one used on the router base in Chapter 2.2 comes from the metal industry and is used to remove the sharp corners on aluminum and mild steel parts. They are inexpensive and easy to use. Draw the sharpened steel tip along the edge of your part, and a thin curl of plastic will be removed. The cutting tip pivots freely to follow edges and only removes a small amount with each pass. Make multiple passes to remove more of the sharp corner. This technique is easy to learn.

If you do not have a deburring tool on hand, a small steel ruler works well too. This technique is also easy to master. A new ruler with a square edge works best. Hold the ruler across the edge you want to scrape and draw it along, leaning it in the direction you are scraping. This is very effective on straight edges, and with practice, you can follow curves as well. It is not quite as efficient as the dedicated deburring tool or scraper but works in a pinch when needed.

Sanding and scraping tools can quickly ease the sharp edges of cut plastics.

Any steel with a clean square edge can be used to scrape both hard and soft plastics.

2. **Create a frosted-edge effect by sanding the scraped edges with a fine grit.** Sponge sanding blocks like the one shown here work well and are flexible enough to sand the softened edges at the same time. If you want the edges to remain square, fine-grit sandpaper wrapped around a solid block will treat the flat edge without rounding the corners. With acrylic, 220-grit sandpaper will produce a nice frost effect on the narrow edge. Working down through finer grits can begin to approach a polished edge, but we want a frosted edge here. The acrylic part is now ready for painting using the stencil from Chapter 1.3.

4.2

NAPKIN HOLDER EDGE

While many projects will only need basic edge treatment, others will need to be polished to transparency, such as the plastic body of this napkin holder. Following the steps used for the sanded edges of the Skyline Window Hanger in Chapter 4.1, we will now finish the edges of the Napkin Holder Parts from Chapter 3.4 to be transparent.

There are two main routes for achieving transparency: buffing or polishing with flame. There are pros and cons for each method. Read through both options first before choosing what works best for you, your workshop, and your particular project.

The acrylic body of these napkin holders look best with fully polished edges.

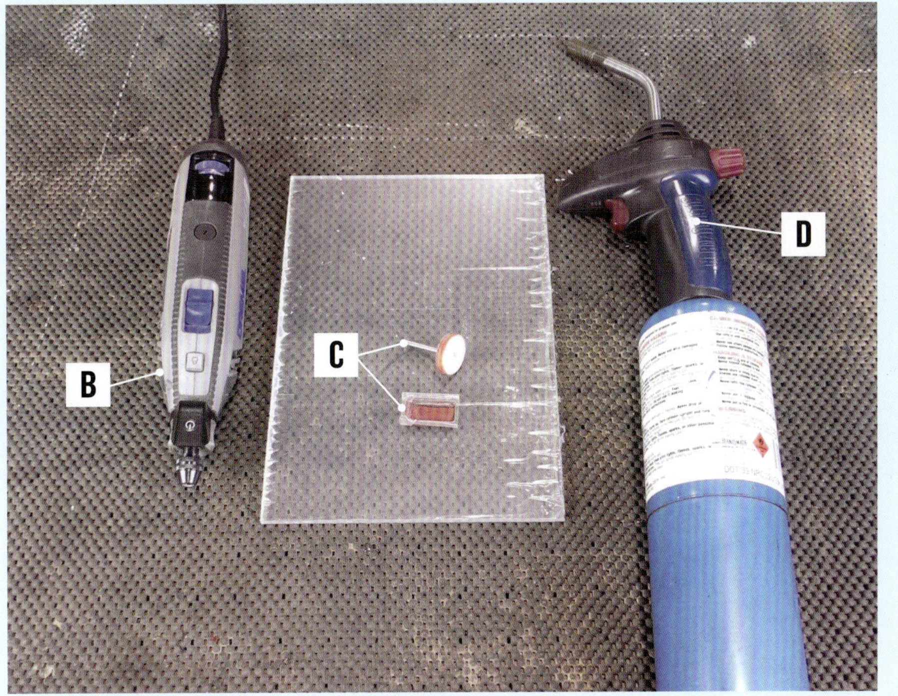

Highly polished edges can be created with tools found in most DIY shops and garages.

Supplies:

- **A.** Acrylic napkin holder from Chapter 3.4
- **B.** Rotary tool
- **C.** Buffing wheel and compound
- **D.** Propane torch (optional)
- **E.** Supplies from Chapter 4.1

1. **Examine the edge of the acrylic.** If you are using the right blade and cutting techniques, it should be sharp and chip free, but you will likely see some tool marks along the edge depending on how you cut it. Start with the techniques from Chapter 4.1 to get the edges initially cleaned up and sanded.

2. **Ready the edges for polishing by sanding them.** Sanding for polishing requires a finer finish than the frosted look of the Skyline Window Hanger. Start sanding with 120 or even 150 grit; your edges should be mostly smooth already. Smoother edges require less work to polish them clear. Work down through the grits as needed to get a uniform look along all the edges to be polished. Sand the radiused corners, as they too will be polished. Sand single pieces by hand, especially with thin stock. A power sander can be too aggressive for a narrow surface.

Sanding Multiple Pieces

Practicing techniques like this stack-sanding process, using scraps, will help you get better and more consistent results.

Stack multiple parts together to sand their edges. This technique saves a lot of time when many of the same parts are needed, like dividers for a tray. Leave the protective film on the parts if possible or use tissue paper between bare faces. Even the dust from sanding can scratch clear plastic if it gets between the faces. Hold the stack vertically when sanding the edges. A thick stack makes it easier to control the sander. Vibrating pad sanders actually work better for this than random orbit sanders.

Lean the stack to the side once the edges are smooth to expose the sharp corners. Run the sander flat across the top of the exposed corners to "break" the sharp edges. Again, be wary of letting unprotected faces rub together. Use a lower speed and a light touch when sanding; heat can build up very quickly under a power sander. Variable speed sanders are very useful here. Lean the stack to the other side and finish sanding the edges. With many parts of the same size, these stacking techniques will save a lot of time in the finishing.

OPTION 1: BUFFING

3. **Buff sanded edges to polish them to a clear shine.** Cloth buffing wheels in the drill press or on a bench stand can be useful. Rotary tools often come with buffing wheels as part of the kit. These will work, but their small size makes them a bit slow. Apply polishing compound on the buffing wheel and watch the edge carefully as you work. Keep RPMs low and move the wheel constantly as you work the edge. Watch for the edge to become smoother as you pass back and forth.

4. **Wipe the edge with a clean cloth regularly.** This is to remove the polishing compound and check the clarity of the edge. Buffing actually heats the edge so that a thin layer of the plastic flows into a smooth surface, making it clear. This process takes time and patience but requires no more specialized equipment than a rotary tool. Practicing on scraps will help you develop the skill. Curves can be buffed, but tighter radii will require smaller wheels. This is where the rotary tool is most useful.

OPTION 2: FLAME

3. **Pass the flame quickly along the well-sanded edges until you get a uniformly smooth, clear edge.** Melt the top layer of the plastic edge without distorting or warping the rest of the part; overheating acrylic can cause bubbles to form under the surface, ruining the edge. Just as with buffing, the goal is to melt the surface layer of the plastic so it flows together into a smooth skin. Flame polishing can be very fast, but it's riskier. Like painting, make each pass without stopping or changing direction. You can always go back to polish more, but flame damage will be hard to fix.

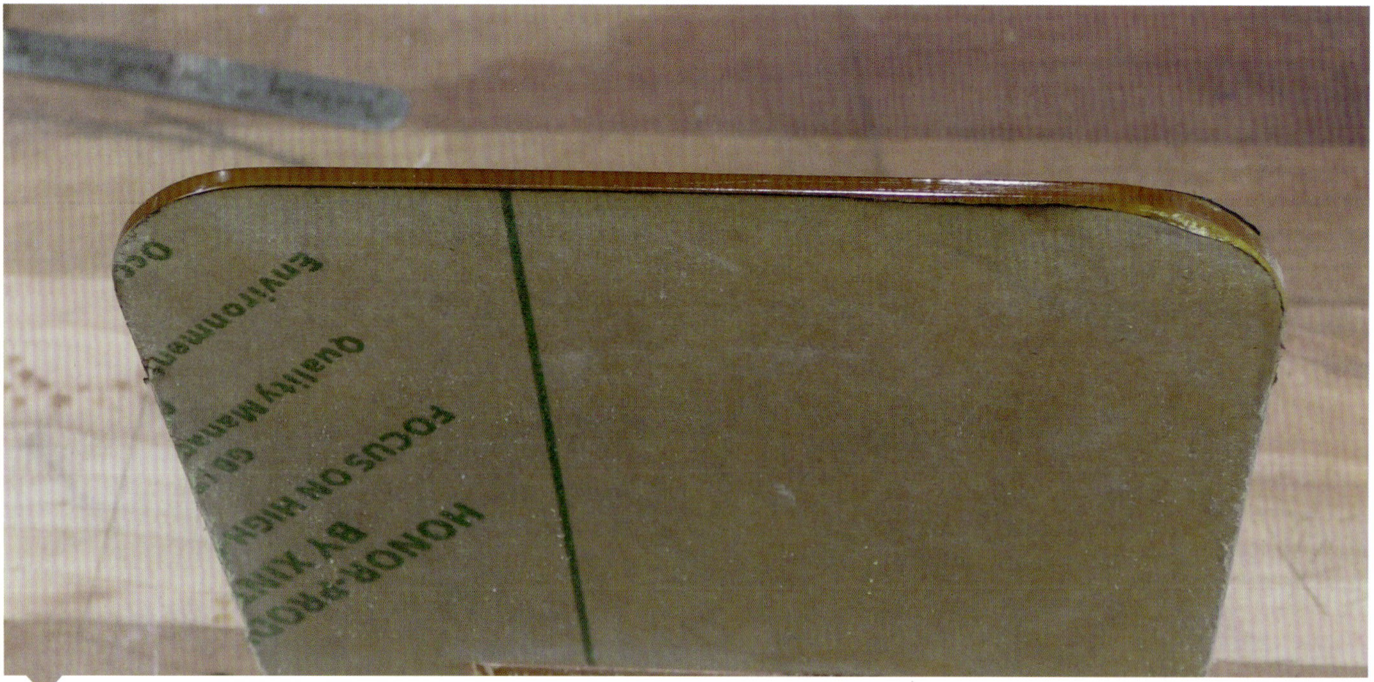

4. **Peel back plastic and paper film away from edges to be flame polished.** The paper can char, leaving soot, and the plastic film can fuse into the polished edge, making it hard to remove. As with buffing, practicing on scraps will let you develop a feel for the flame you are using and how to work with different plastics. Any flame can be used, but care must be taken to avoid soot contaminating the edges.

5. **Stack multiple parts together horizontally to flame their edges as a set.** Align the prepared edges together along the edge of your work surface. Use a surface that you do not mind getting scorched. Run the flame side to side, passing beyond the edge of the stack before reversing direction. This is very similar to the right technique for spray painting. Work down the stack as you pass the flame side to side. If you miss any spots, they will be easy to see, and you can simply pass over them again. Practice the technique and you will be able to polish a lot of parts in a short time.

The Cleanest Flame

Some form of soot is a byproduct of most combustion, and the propane torch used in Chapter 4.2 produces some soot. It's not easily visible, but it is there. The exception to this is a hydrogen/oxygen flame. Combining hydrogen and oxygen in a flame produces H_2O (water vapor)—no soot involved. This book is about working plastics with common woodshop tools, so a standard propane torch works really well. But if you happen to find yourself polishing a lot of plastic, you can use an oxy-acetylene torch. Connect it to a bottle of oxygen and another of hydrogen to get flames that are hot enough to polish parts very quickly with no soot.

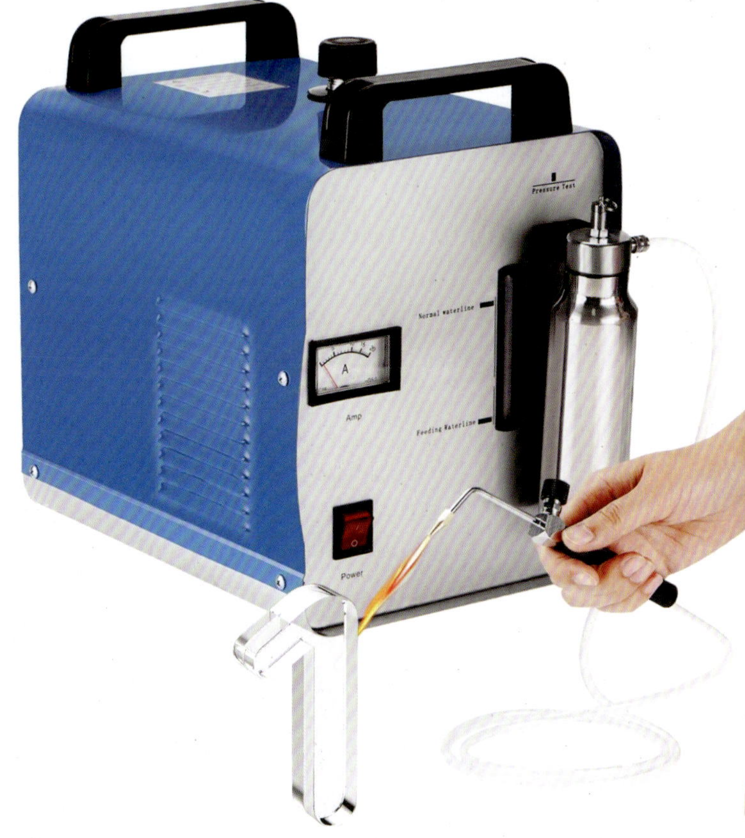

Hydrogen generators break down water into hydrogen and oxygen gas for the torch. This is easier than keeping bottle gas.

5

Chapter 5: Fabrication Techniques

Plastics are often produced and used as single-part items, but you will find occasions to assemble parts. There are several options, including glues, welding, and mechanical fasteners.

5.1 ROUTER EDGE GUIDE

Most plastics can be drilled and tapped for threads like metals can be. Both soft and brittle plastics can be threaded with standard taps. Soft plastics like nylon and polycarbonate can be fastened with blind rivets, though acrylic will usually crack or break as the rivets are set.

Polycarbonate is excellent for mechanical fastening, as it can take great strain, is shock resistant, and holds threads nearly as well as aluminum in my experience. It is the right material to use for this adjustable edge guide for my shop-built offset router base. This edge guide features two adjustable fences with rollers that allow it to be set up to follow straight or curved edges.

The parts for this edge guide were CNC cut, but in the original one I built many years ago, they were made by hand. A polycarbonate sheet with a 1/4" (6mm) thickness was used in both cases. Pilot holes were drilled at the CNC where all the mechanical fasteners needed to be.

Plastic parts can be made into working assemblies with mechanical fasteners.

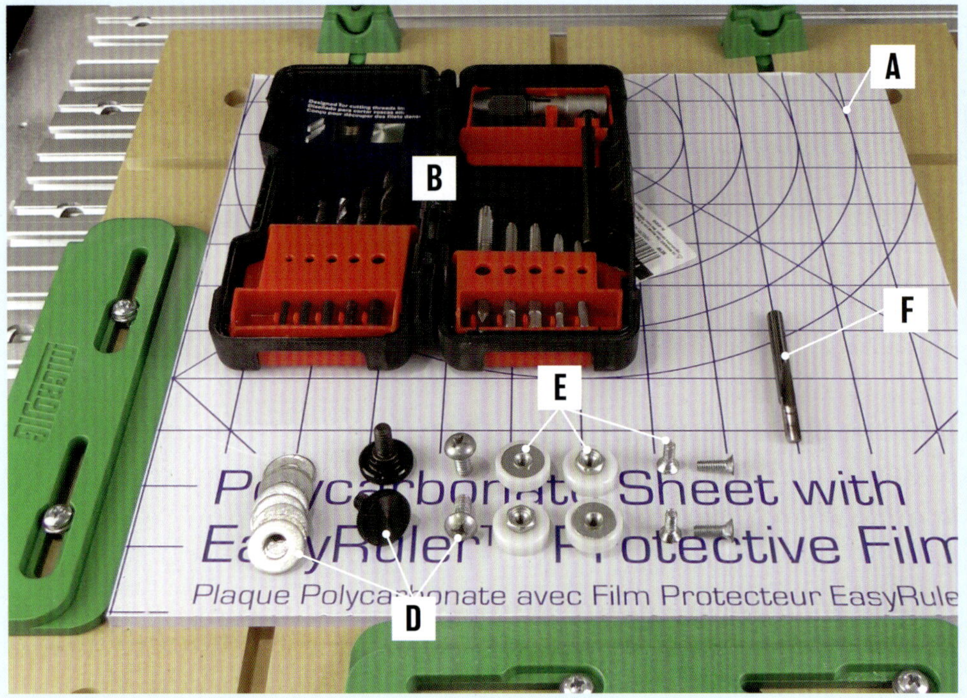

Working in wood, plastic, or metals, every shop should have a good basic set of taps and know how to use them.

Supplies:

- **A.** Polycarbonate sheet, 0.22" (6mm) thick
- **B.** Drill and tap set (decimal or metric)
- **C.** Countersink
- **D.** 1/4-20 (M6 x 1) and 10-32 (M4 x 0.75) hardware
- **E.** Closet door roller wheels
- **F.** 1/4" (6mm) router bit

1. **Drill out the pilot holes with the proper bit for the tap to be used.** For the 1/4-20 threads, use a #7 drill bit. For the M6 x 1 tap, use a 5mm bit. The bits here are part of the tap set and have not been reground for plastic use (see "Upgrading Drill Bits" on page 58). The flexible polycarbonate drills easily and there is little chance of breaking with these standard twist drill bits. It should be noted that while bits with a typical 118- or 153-degree tip generally work well in plastics, brad point bits are simply not suitable and should not be used in any type of plastic

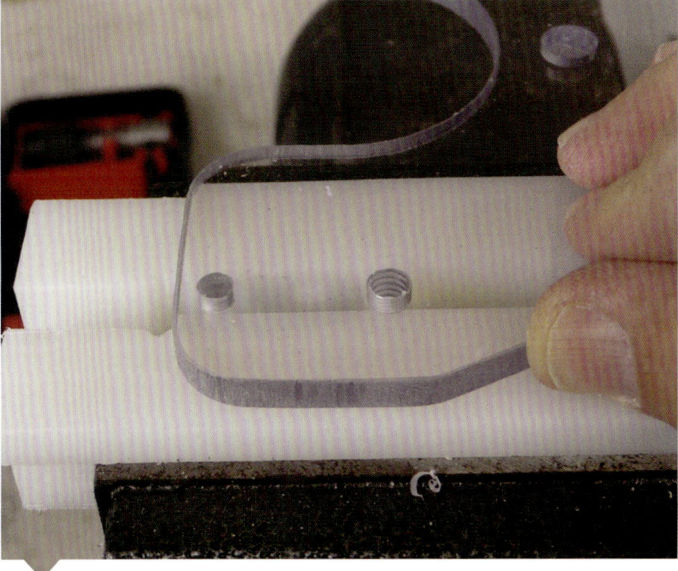

2. **Tap the holes with the 1/4-20 (M6 x 1) tap.** You can use the hand chuck that comes in the tap set, but plastics tap easily enough that you can use a driver on low speed. You do not need any sort of lubricant when tapping soft or hard plastics. As with tapping metal or wood, it is important to start the tap as close to perpendicular to the pilot hole as possible. A tap is fully capable of cutting threads at a different angle to the hole. The trick is to start straight and let the tapered tip of the tap find the center line as it advances.

3. **Countersink holes in the adjustable fences.** The 10-32 (M4 x 0.75) flat head screws that will hold the wheels need to be inside the polycarbonate so they clear the body when the fences are set up for curves. A typical woodworking countersink works fine on plastic. The one shown is for wood and features a single cutting flute. It scrapes the countersink angle into the plastic quite well without too much heat. I have used countersinks with multiple flutes designed for metal. They cut plastics just fine, but the multiple cutting teeth do generate more friction, so keep the speed low and watch the heat.

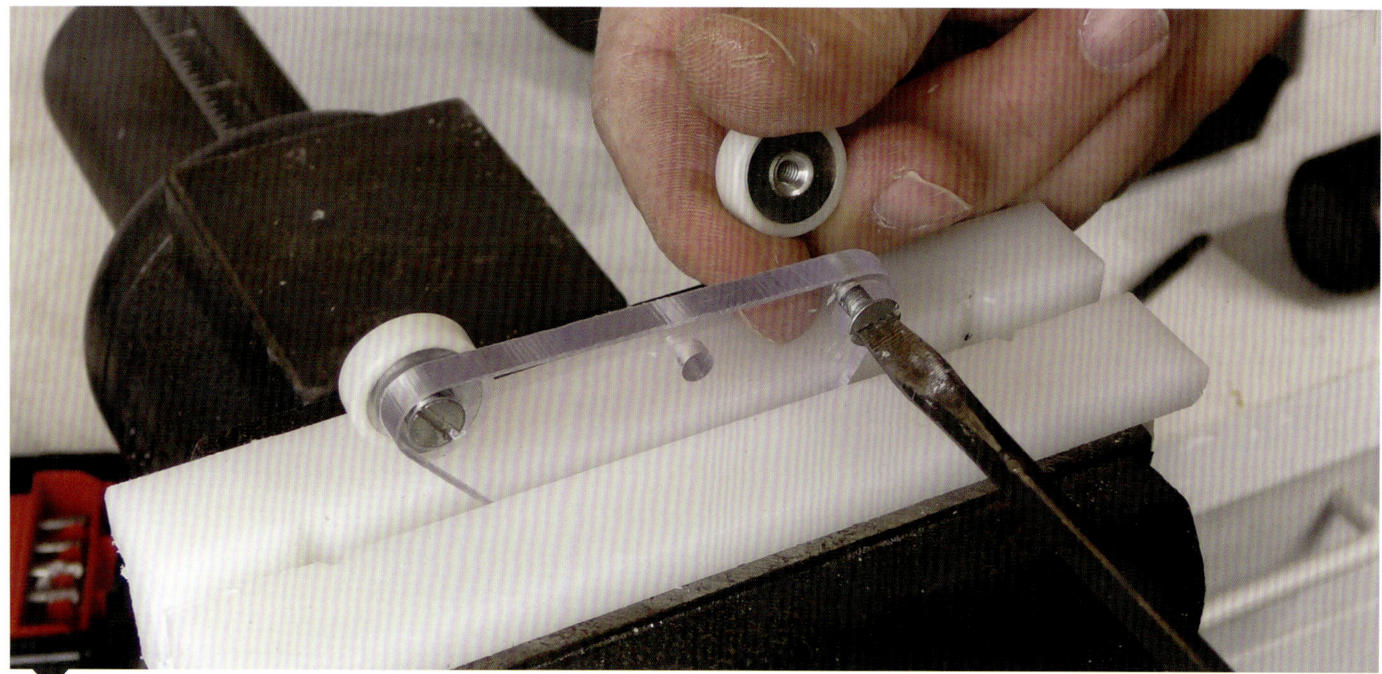

4. **Attach the roller wheels to the fences.** The rollers here are for shower doors. They can be bought as replacements at hardware stores and home centers. They feature a threaded bearing in the center, so they are easy to attach with the flat head screws. The nylon vise jaws from Chapter 2.3 are being used to gently hold these parts without damage as they are worked. The "tires" on the rollers are also nylon and will not mark your wood project as they guide the router.

5. **This shop-built edge guide shows off some of the mechanical fastening options you have when working with plastics.** Here, there are screws that hold the fences onto the body and let them pivot. Locking fluid was applied on assembly to keep them from loosening in use. The hand knobs that hold the fences in position will be tightened and loosened with almost every use of the edge guide. My experience has shown that these threads in the polycarbonate will last for many years of use.

5.2 NAPKIN HOLDER DECORATION

Plastics that can be solvent bonded like styrenes, acrylics, and polycarbonates can be easily decorated with applied ornaments. These can be stickers, silkscreens, pad prints, or appliqués. The napkin holder from Chapters 3.4 and 4.2 gets some mid-century modern flair with a couple of simple plastic parts glued on. For the acrylics that are being used with the napkin holder, two basic forms of solvent glue are available: a thicker tube glue and a water-thin liquid glue. Since the appliqués are opaque, the tube glue is easier to use.

Note: The napkin holder must be thermoformed on the strip bender in Chapter 6.4 before you decorate and assemble it in this chapter.

Simple contrasting appliqués add a new level of design style to your projects.

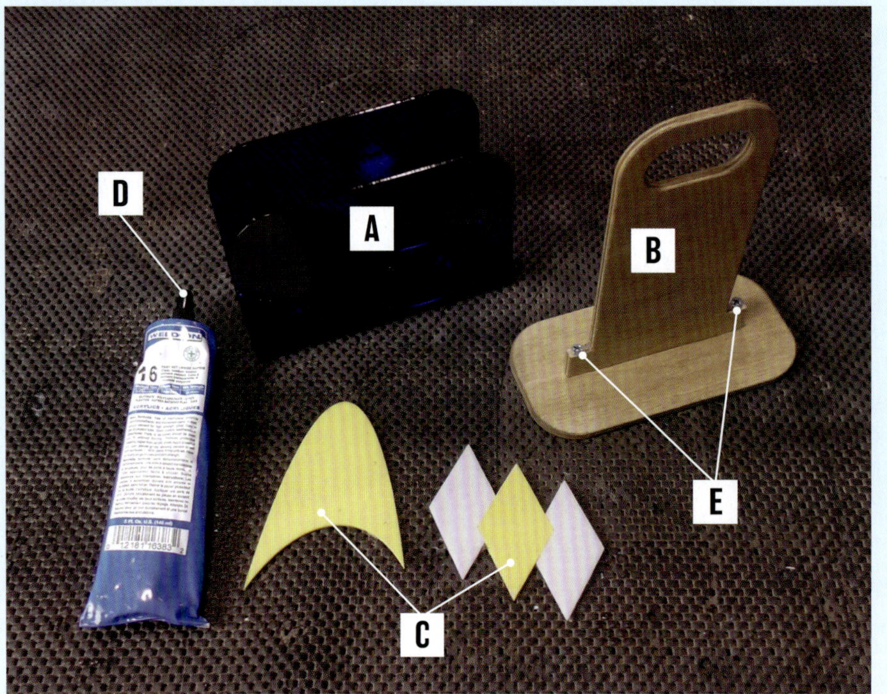

This assembly just needs a few parts, some glue, and a couple of screws.

Supplies:

- **A.** Acrylic napkin holder from Chapter 6.4
- **B.** Plywood napkin base from Chapter 3.4
- **C.** Acrylic parts for appliqués
- **D.** Tube solvent cement
- **E.** #4 wood screws, 1/2" (12mm) long

1. **Clean all the plastic surfaces that will be bonded.** The protective film can be left on the appliqué pieces and removed just before applying the glue. Use a mild glass cleaner or specialty plastic cleaner (see Chapter 5.6) to clean the faces of the napkin holder if needed. Assemble the plywood napkin base if it's not already constructed.

2. **Apply cement sparingly to the back side of the appliqué.** You need to apply enough to form a solid bond but not so much that it will squeeze out. There is no good way to clean up any that comes out of the edges where it will show.

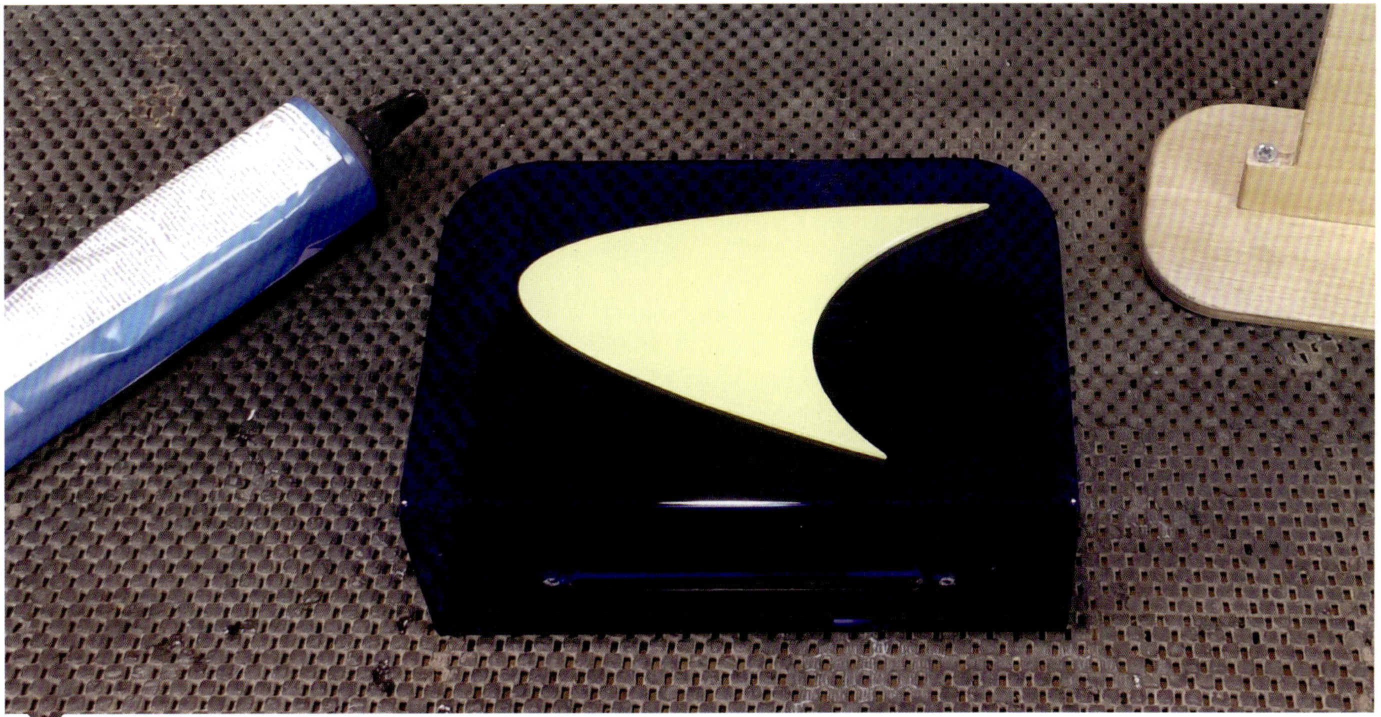

3. **Attach the appliqué.** Set the holder flat on the work surface, position the appliqué where you want it on the face, and gently press it in place. It should not move once pressed in place. Let it set for at least 10 minutes before touching the parts or follow the time recommended by the manufacturer for your cement.

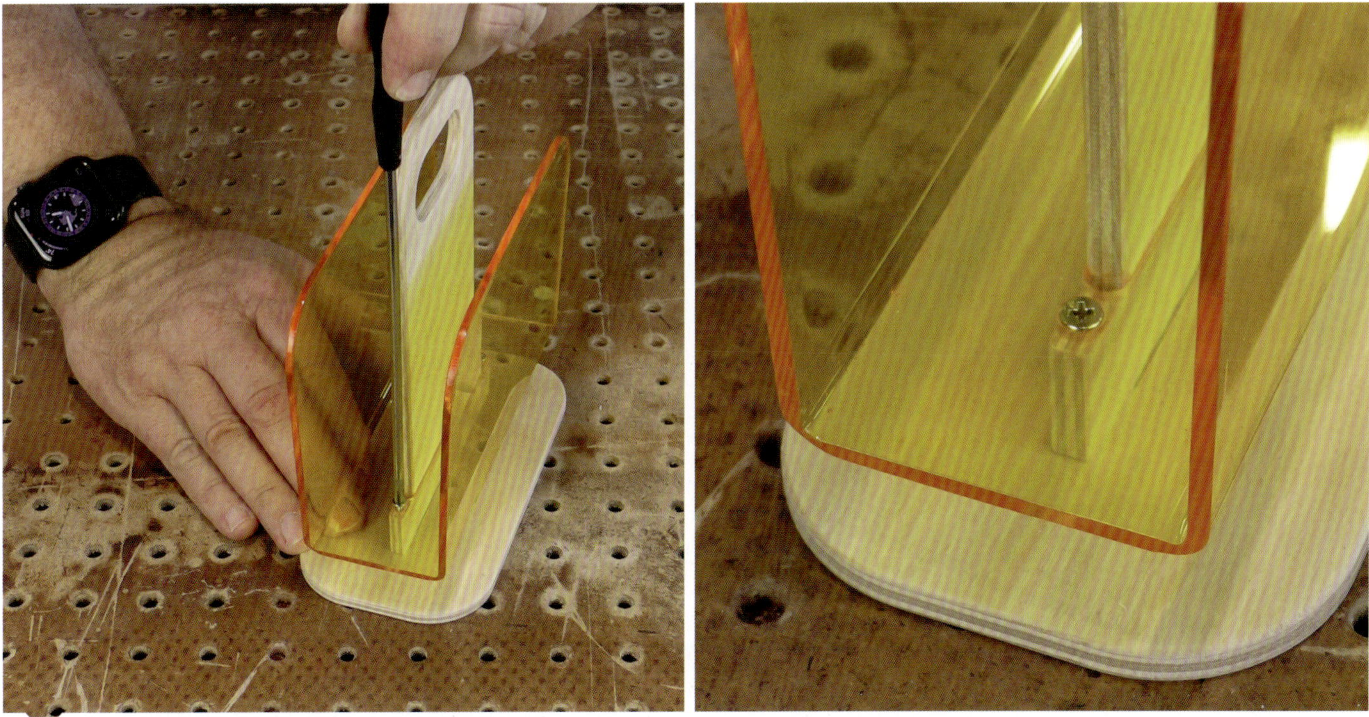

4. **Secure the napkin holder to the base with #4 wood screws.** There is no good way to glue the small plywood base to the flat acrylic, so the connection is best made mechanically with screws. This is why the napkin holder part was made with countersunk screw holes. You may need to drill pilot holes in the plywood upright to accept the screws.

5.3

BUSINESS CARD HOLDER

The card holder here is made of clear acrylic, which means the glue joints will be visible through the face of the clear sides. The thick tube glue used in Chapter 5.2 will not work well for this; water-thin solvent cement is available that can be applied to joints that are dry fitted in place. The thin liquid wicks into a properly made joint through **capillary action**. For example, this is what causes spilled water to flow all the way under your tablet as it sits on the table. Knowing how capillary action works allows for making the very clean joints that are required in clear plastic assemblies.

Note: The body of the card holder must be thermoformed on the strip bender in Chapter 6.3 before you assemble it in this chapter. However, start in this chapter to cut the parts first.

Clear plastic sides require clean and uniform glue joints.

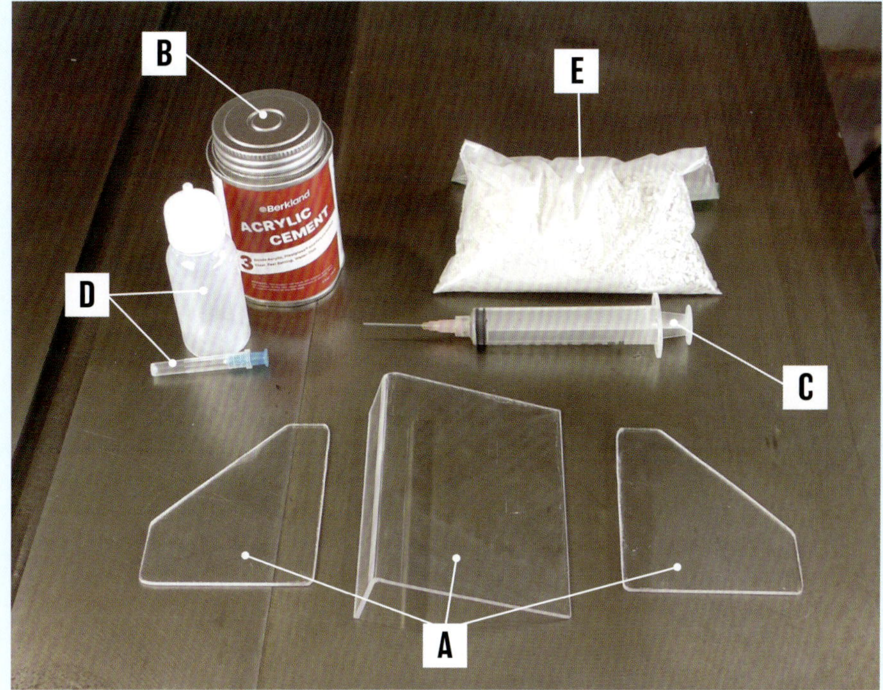

Applicators are ideal for applying liquid glue to clear parts.

Supplies:

- **A.** Clear acrylic sheet, 0.08" (2mm) thick (including body from Chapter 6.3)
- **B.** Water-thin solvent cement
- **C.** Plastic glue syringe
- **D.** Glue applicator bottle (optional)
- **E.** Sandbags
- **F.** Scoring tool

1. **Prepare the parts to be assembled.** This holder is made up of three simple parts: two shaped sides and the body, which will be thermoformed in Chapter 6.3. The body is cut to 3-3/4" (95mm) wide x 4" (100mm) long. The sides start at 2-1/2" (64mm) wide x 3" (75mm) tall. Cut the sides to a triangular shape as shown. The angles on these side parts are too large for easy cutting with a miter gauge, but they can be scored and snapped easily. The two halves should be as similar as possible, but a tiny difference in this angled front edge will not be noticeable.

Sand and smooth all four sides of the body. Ease the edges slightly as you do. Polish the 3-3/4" (95mm) top and bottom edges only, leaving the 4" (100mm) sides smooth but unpolished. Polished edges cannot be solvent glued without cracking.

2.

Thermoform the body in Chapter 6.3. The body will need to be heated on the strip bender and formed into the L shape before continuing. Check the bend on the body. There can often be some spreading at the bend line that extends slightly beyond the edge of the part. If found, sand this flat so the L-shaped body will sit flat on the sides for gluing.

3.

4.

Set up on a clean, smooth, and flat surface. A granite setup plate is ideal, but a cast-iron table saw top like the one here works well. The edges and faces to be glued must not have the protective film near the joint line; the glue will wick underneath the film if it comes in contact. Position the body of the card holder onto one of the sides where you want to glue it. Visually check and ensure that there are no gaps along the joint. Parts are typically aligned along an edge, but here the body is positioned within the borders of the side part. Apply glue one side at a time. Production setups can be fixtured to glue both sides at the same time, but the glue sets up so quickly that it is not usually necessary.

5. **Hold the body in place with a light weight.** The body will slide quite easily across the side part, so a small sandbag balanced across the upper edge of the body will hold it in place as the glue is applied. A simple plastic bag filled with play sand is sufficient. These parts are small, so the bag should be too. Larger sandbags can be used for larger assemblies.

6. **Fill your applicator with the solvent cement.** This glue included an applicator bottle and needle, but I find that a disposable glue syringe offers much better control. With no air inside, the solvent only flows as you press lightly on the plunger. The bottle will have air inside that can allow the solvent to drip where it will leave marks on any plastic it hits.

Glue Joint Precautions

Edges that will be glued should not be polished or heat treated to avoid stress cracking caused by the solvent.

The process of polishing plastic edges by buffing or flame involves lightly melting the surface so it flows into a smooth surface. This looks good, but the heating process introduces stress into the edges. Typically, this is not an issue, but if solvent is applied to polished edges, the stress will form cracks. These very fine fissures are known as crazing, and once they appear, there is no fix.

To avoid this, make sure that edges being glued are sanded and/or scraped smooth, but not polished. The solvent will flow into the joint and melt the plastic edge before it evaporates. Done properly, the joint will become clear anyway, so polishing does not make it better and can ruin the project.

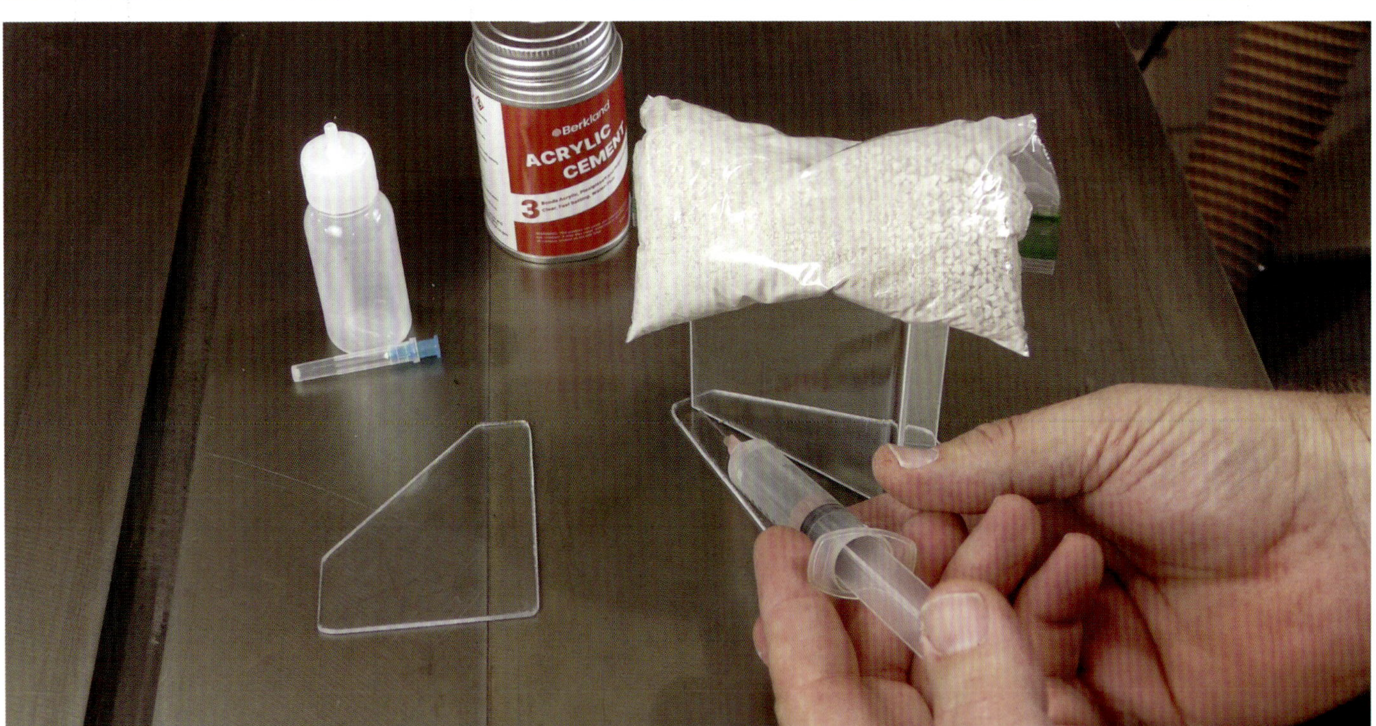

7. **Apply the solvent along the joint.** Capillary action will automatically draw the thin liquid into the joint between the two parts. You will be able to clearly see the refraction of the plastic change as the joint fills. Apply the solvent only fast enough to let it fill the joint without pooling next to the plastic. Typically, I apply the solvent from the back or underside of the joint. This will show excess solvent less. The needle is drawn lightly along the joint. The sandbag keeps the body from moving, but you need a light touch here. Wait for the joint to dry before moving anything. The parts can be carefully handled to continue assembly after about 30 seconds, but the joint will not be fully cured for a few hours. Check the manufacturer's recommendations for whatever brand solvent you are using.

8. **Align the second joint to be glued in the same manner.** If the body was being applied along an edge of the sides, this would be simple; but because it is inside the edges of the side part, the two sides must be aligned before gluing. I used a couple of squares on my table saw top to line up the joinery after setting the sandbag on top. You can also use shop-built fixtures (like the ones in Chapter 5.4) to align the sides.

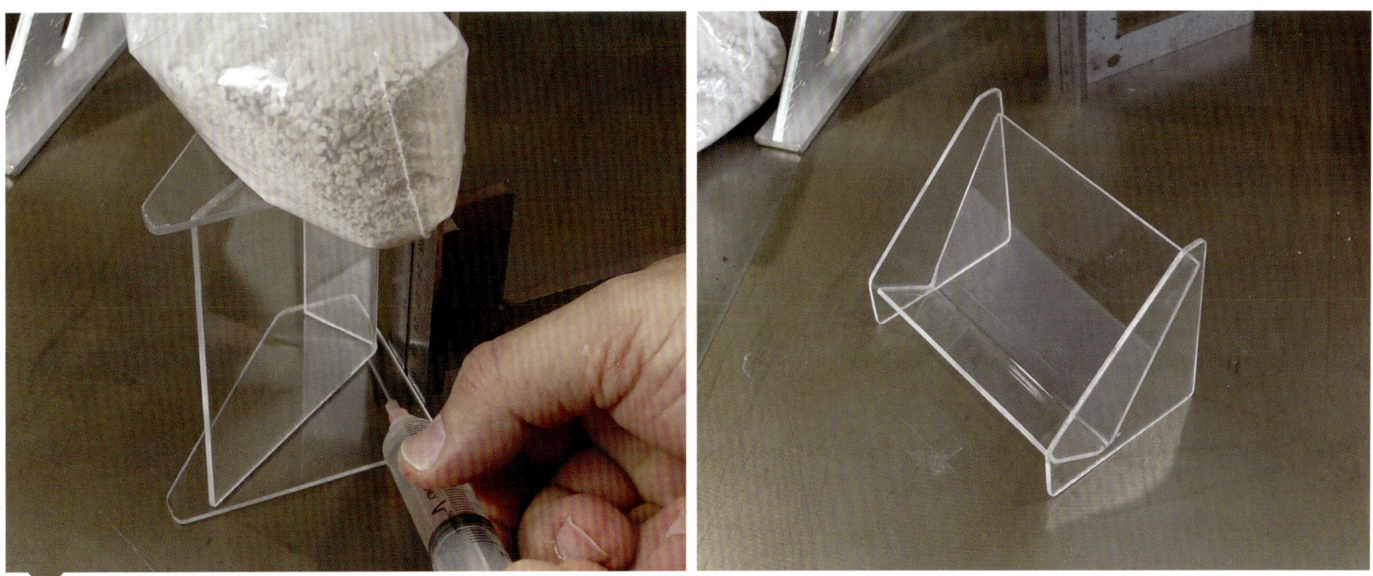

9. **Repeat steps 5–7 on the second side.** If you have aligned the parts correctly, the card holder should sit flat when set on the table. This gluing technique is not difficult but does require a light touch to ensure a good joint without getting glue all over the parts. It is useful to practice bonding some small scraps together first to gain a feel for how it all works.

5.4
CORNER JOINTS

Using the water-thin solvent cement (as shown in Chapter 5.3) is the preferred method for gluing clear plastics, and like the tube cement (as shown in Chapter 5.2), it only works with acrylic and polycarbonate. But it sets up rapidly, so even complex assemblies can be completed at a reasonable pace. The full build of boxes, bins, and dispensers would fill their own book and are beyond the scope of this one, but this is a good chance to demonstrate the basic joints.

The corner joint being created here is representative of many hundreds of plastic containers that I used to fabricate when I worked at Eastern Plastics Company: two sides joined together into a corner and fixed on a bottom. With the right setup, all the seams between the three parts can be glued at the same time. As in Chapter 5.3, the work must be done on a smooth, flat surface.

Thicker parts are still bonded using capillary action to fill the joint with solvent, but the thicker the stock, the more accurately the parts need to be dry fitted for this to work. The 1/4" (6mm) parts being glued into a sample corner joint here need to be supported by shop-built glue fixtures as they are worked.

This corner joint is so clear that you can see the saw marks from the other end of the plastic.

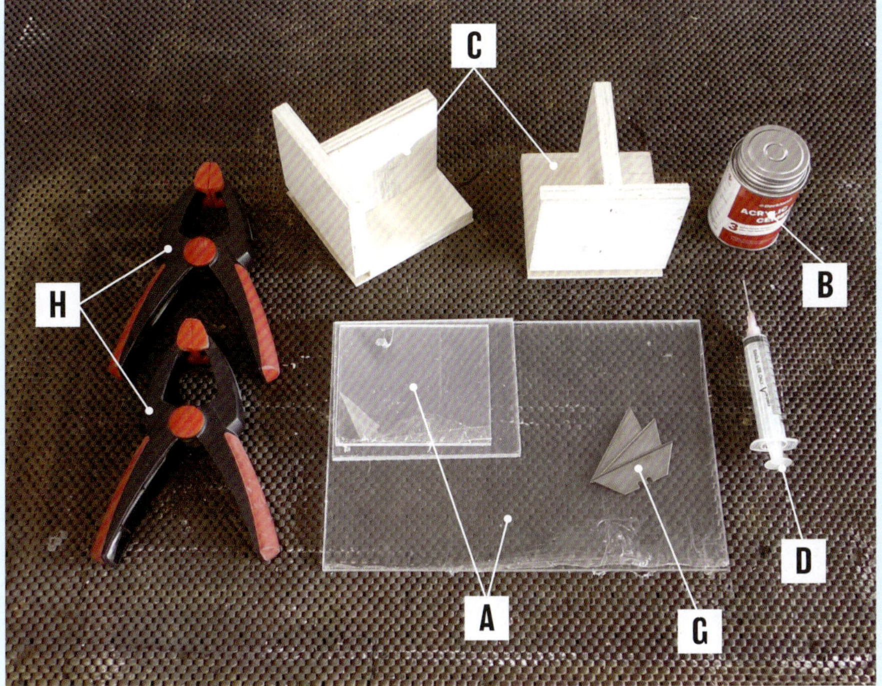

Many of the same items used in Chapter 5.4 are also used for thicker plastic stock.

Supplies:

- A. Acrylic sheet, 0.25" (6mm) thick
- B. Water-thin solvent cement
- C. Glue fixtures (see sidebar on page 104)
- D. Plastic glue syringe
- E. Glue applicator bottle (optional)
- F. Sandbags
- G. Utility knife blades (optional)
- H. Spring clamps
- I. 0.002" (0.05mm) feeler gauge

1. **Position the parts together without glue to prepare all the seams.** The base part lies flat on the surface; the side parts rest along the edges of the base and come together in the vertical corner. The protective film can be removed completely from the parts or peeled back away from the joints. The film helps protect it during the assembly. Just like joining boards together, you need to plan ahead of time which boards overlap and cut them to size accordingly. Generally, you will want the most visible face to overlap the others. These will be butt joints. The process for fabricating solvent-welded miters is museum-quality work and beyond the scope of this book.

2. **Clamp the parts into position so all the seams are aligned square and show no gaps.** The glue fixtures are used here to support the parts. Light-duty spring clamps hold the parts to the supports. If the base does not meet the bottom edge of the sides, it can be wedged up to them using the utility knife blades as very thin wedges. If your surface is flat, this should not be needed.

Shop-Built Glue Fixtures

These are simple 90-degree plywood squares glued and nailed together. There is also a thin plywood part attached to the bottom exactly in line with the upright face. The blocks serve three purposes: holding the sides vertical and perpendicular to the base, aligning the faces of the sides to the edge of the base, and leaving the joint at the base open.

Without the gap at the bottom of the fixture, the thin adhesive could easily wick through the joint and spread between the side and fixture, which would ruin the joint. You can build a simple 90-degree piece and cut a kerf about 1/8" (3mm) up from the bottom, but I used 1/8" (3mm) plywood I had on hand because it will be more durable.

These simple fixtures are easy for any woodshop to make and use.

The base and side must be aligned accurately without the fixture covering the seam.

Visually check and ensure that there are no gaps along the joint. A 0.002" (0.05mm) feeler gauge should just drag lightly between parts. If the gaps are too big, add wedges until the feeler gauge drags. Larger assemblies will require longer seams and will be more challenging.

3.

4. **Apply the solvent cement along all the aligned seams.** Generally, you want to flow glue into the vertical corner seam first, working from top to bottom. The glue will flow down with gravity, and the excess will flow into the seams connected to it as it reaches the bottom. Then glue can be run along the base seams, working from the corner outward. It is always best to work along one direction whenever possible. As the glue flows into the joint, it displaces any air in the seam. So, working along the seam toward a filled area can trap bubbles that will be quite visible. The goal is to fill the entire seam between edges without overflowing glue onto the faces of the parts.

Plastic Shapes and Fasteners

One thing that may be surprising is the number and variety of commercially available plastic shapes, parts, and accessories there are. To begin with, styrene like we worked with in Chapter 1 is used extensively in architectural and engineering models, so there are structural shapes you can buy premade. Round or square rods, tubes, and angles in enough variety to build a scale oil refinery are available from the companies that make the sheet stock.

Acrylic and other clear plastic shapes and hardware can also be bought for use. Hinges, latches, corner brackets, jewelry hangers, circles, dowels, and cubes are all available that can be solvent welded to your plastic projects. You can use all of these options in the same ways you use hardware in your woodshop already.

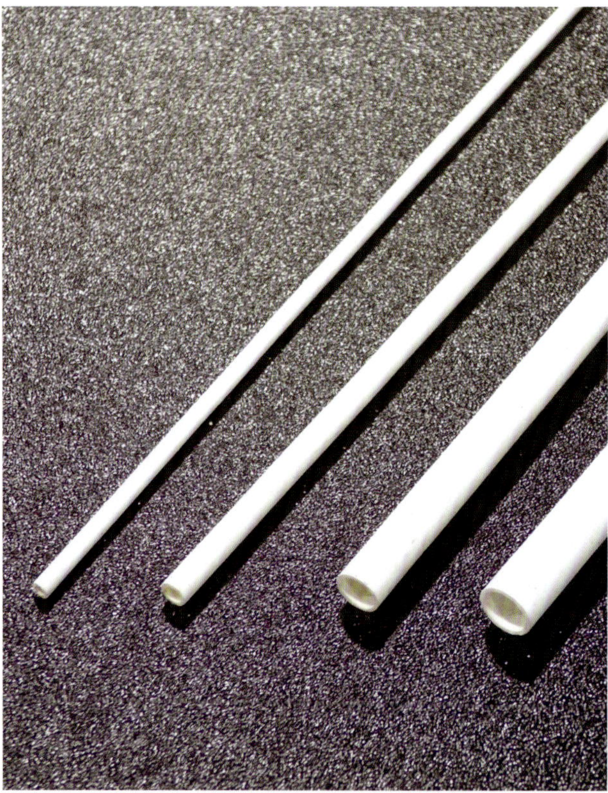

Styrene and ABS tubes, rods, and strips are commonly used in architectural and engineering models.

Plastic accessories are available in shapes, as hardware, and in different plastic types.

5.5

RESTORATION

However carefully you try to work your plastic parts, accidents and mistakes will happen. While sometimes it is better to simply make new parts, plastic is expensive and saving a project that is nearly complete is preferable if possible. Knowing how to make minor repairs, such as polishing out a glue spill on the business card holder from Chapter 5.3, will save materials and time in your shop.

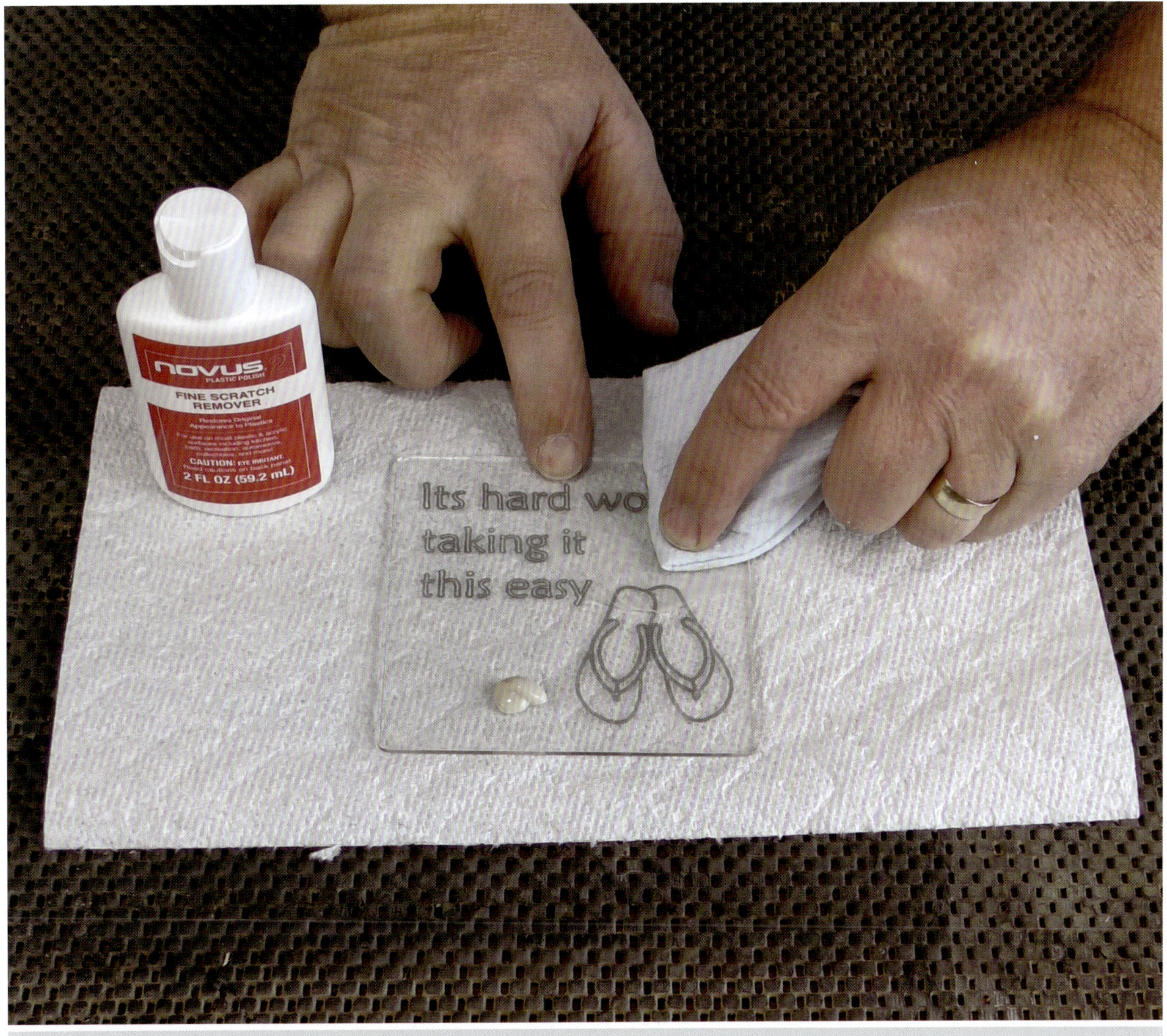

Being able to remove minor damage to your parts can often prevent having to start over.

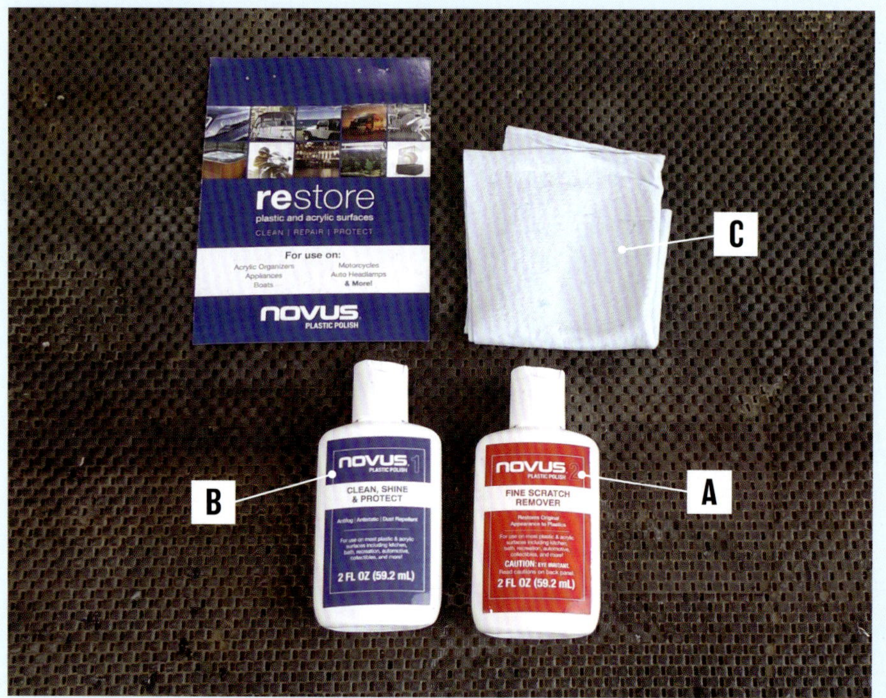

Cleaner and polish are easily available and work very well.

Supplies:

- **A.** Plastic polish
- **B.** Plastic cleaner
- **C.** Microfiber cleaning cloths
- **D.** Toothpaste (optional)

1. **Assess the damage to the part.** Excess glue got on one of the sides of the business card holder (from Chapter 5.3), discoloring the clear plastic. The sign from Chapter 3.5 had very fine scratches in the surface that were hard to see until the part was edge lit, causing them to glow like the engraving. Both can be polished out.

2. **Apply a drop of plastic polish to the damage.** The polish is a light buffing compound, like the one used with the rotary tool in Chapter 4 but mixed with liquid for hand polishing. Shake the bottle to mix any solids that may have settled. Use only enough for the immediate area you are working, or it will dry on the plastic. Surprisingly, toothpaste can be used in a pinch to buff out minor scratches. It contains fine silica very similar to that used in buffing compounds. It is not ideal but can be useful if you just need a quick fix.

3. **Buff the damaged area using a lint-free cloth.** Use a light circular motion centered on the worst of the damage and work outward. This is just like sanding out damage on wood parts: you want to remove the damage then feather the edges out until they fade from view. The polishing compound is an abrasive fine enough to restore the clear surface of the plastic.

Wash away the polish with the plastic cleaner to check your progress. Use a separate cloth from the one with polishing compound on it. Depending on the level of damage, you may need to apply more polish and keep working. Inspect the edges of the work area to ensure that they blend in with the undamaged surface.

4.

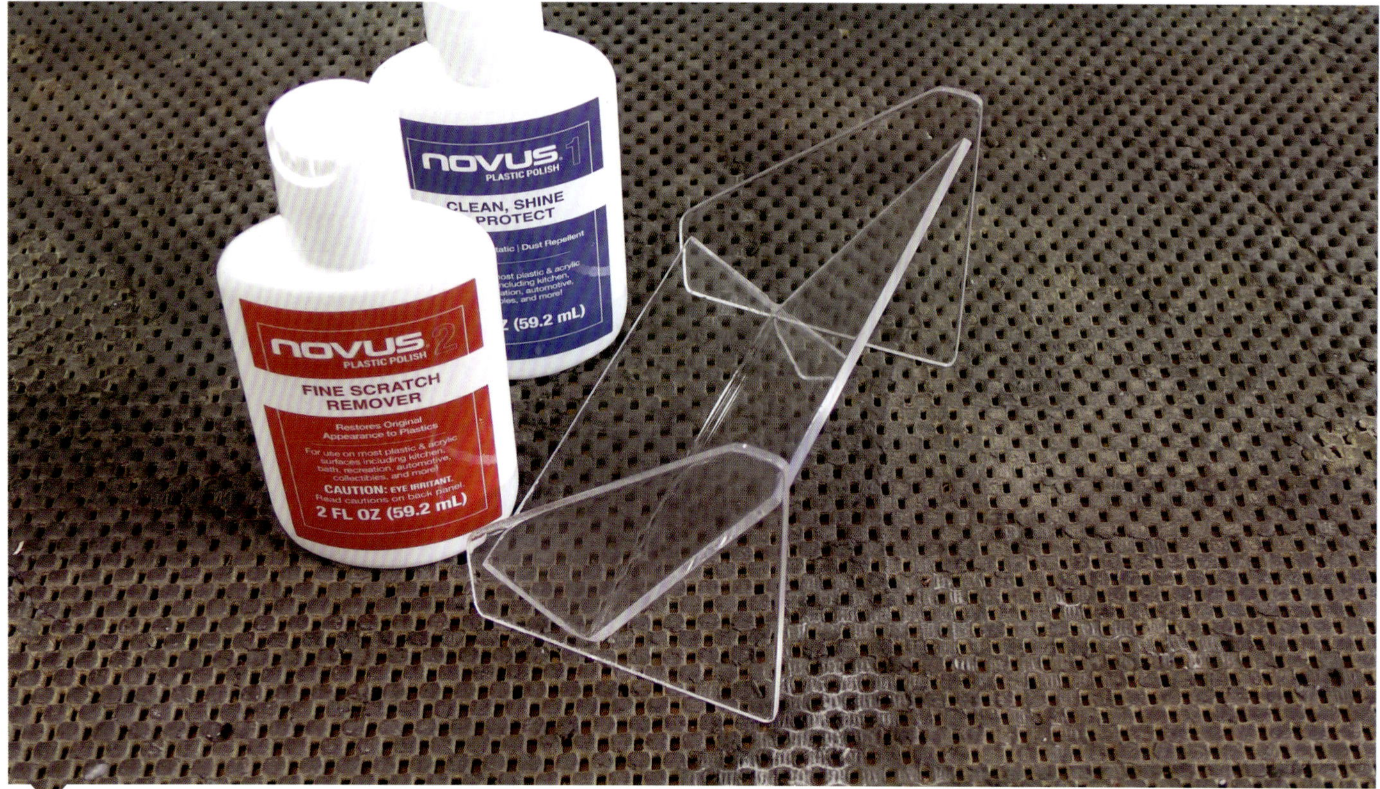

5. **Wipe down the entire part using the plastic cleaner.** This will remove excess polish haze and any fingerprints from handling the part. The plastic cleaner is more effective on plastics than ordinary glass cleaner, and it also reduces static on the surface that can attract dust. I use this to clean plastic glazing (see Chapter 2.1) before fixing it onto the artwork. The repair process does take time, but you will likely be surprised by how well it works. If you did not know where the glue originally was on the card holder, you might not be able to find it now.

Thermal Welding

Thermal welding of some plastics is possible with the proper equipment.

While many plastics cannot be solvent welded, they can be "welded" with the right equipment. The process is very similar to welding metals: the edges to be welded are clamped in place, and a rod of plastic is melted into the joint where it fuses the sheet edges together before cooling.

The equipment and techniques are rarely used in casual plastic working, as this book is meant to teach, but I wanted to include the information here in case a reader wanted to explore more involved plastic fabrication.

6

Chapter 6: Plastic Forming

Many types of sheet plastics can be shaped with simple bends. Depending on the type of plastic, this can be done mechanically without heat, by heating the plastic, or a combination of both. This chapter will showcase these techniques.

6.1

ROUTER BIT GUARD COLD FORM

The router table bit guard from Chapter 3.2 needs to be bent to form the guard that extends over the bit. The thin polycarbonate can be bent to shape without heat, using a process called **cold forming**. The process works best for practical projects over decorative ones. Cold forming is simple and requires no special tools but will not produce bends that look as nice as **thermoforming** will.

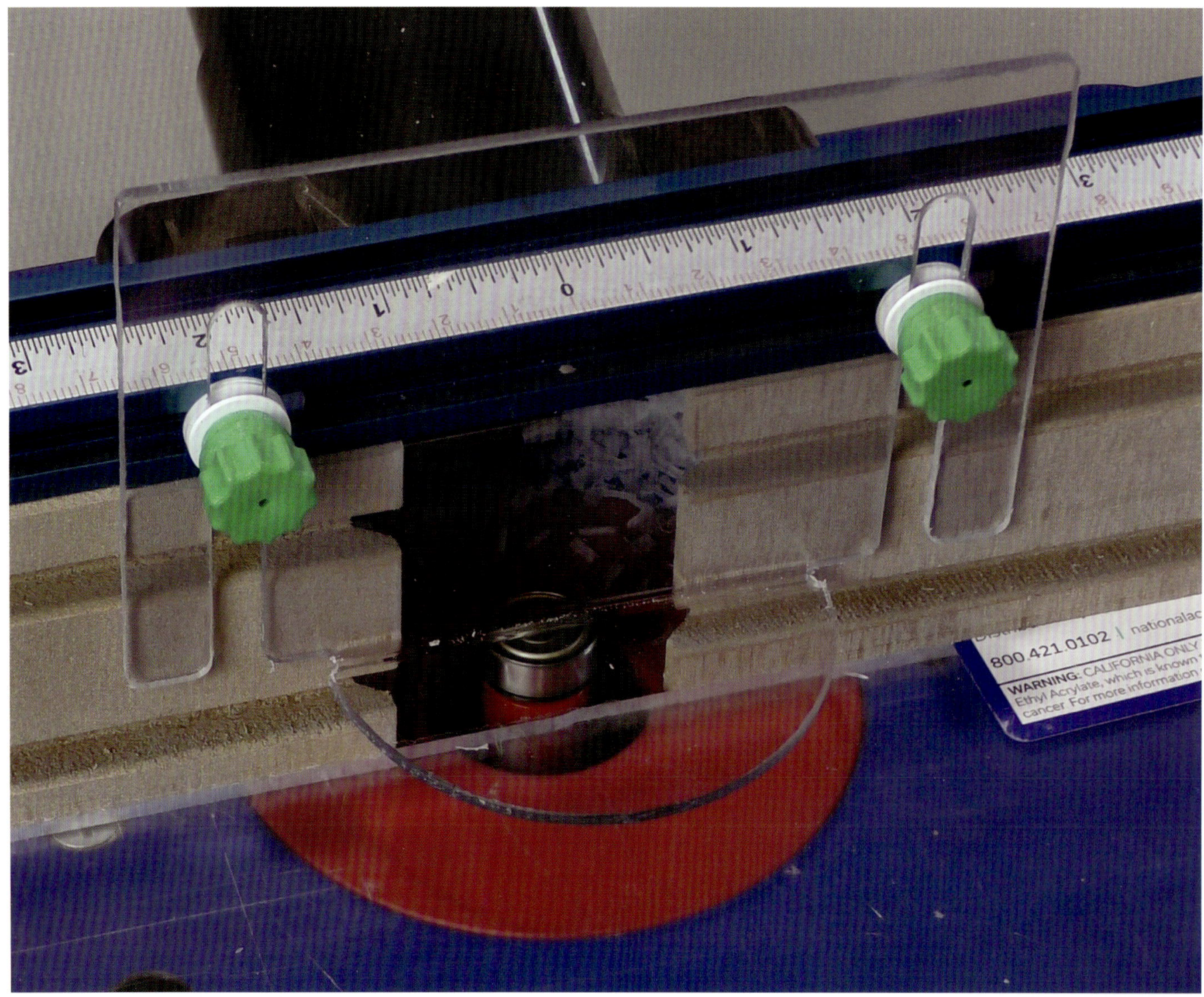

This sort of cold forming can also be done using a sheet metal brake.

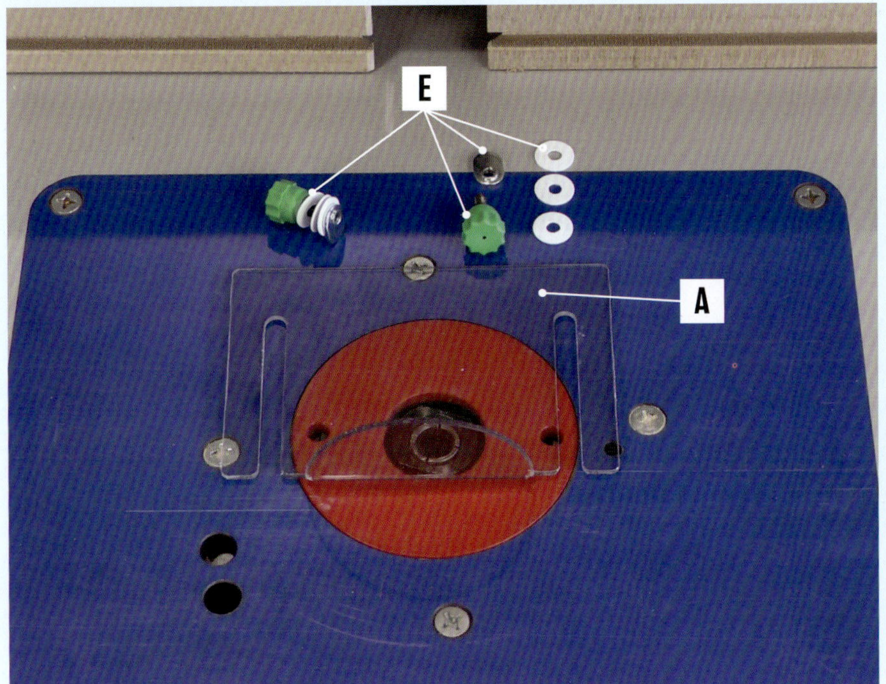

The hardware for attaching the bit guard will be determined by your router table fence. Thumb screws with weld nuts worked for my table.

Supplies:

- **A.** Polycarbonate bit guard blank from Chapter 3.2
- **B.** Vise
- **C.** HDPE vice jaws from Chapter 2.3
- **D.** Mallet or hammer
- **E.** Bit guard hardware
- **F.** Heat gun (optional)

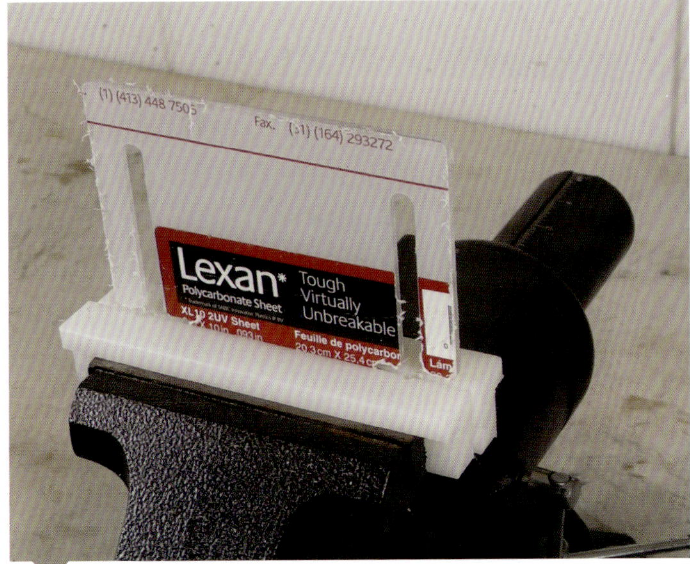

1. **Clamp the bit guard blank in a vise.** The bend point needs to be aligned with the top of the jaws. Remember that the blank was made with bend line indicators milled in to help this alignment. The soft jaws will hold the blank securely without scratching as it is bent. Leaving the protective film in place will also help to protect the part.

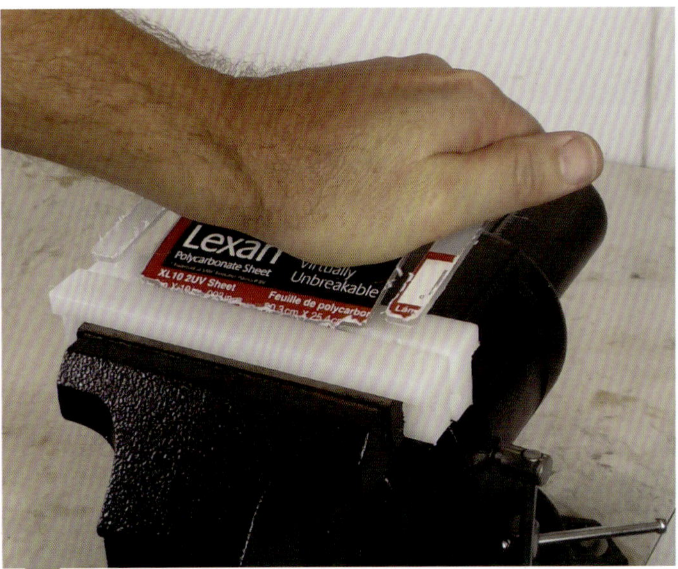

2. **Bend the body of the guard by hand as far as possible.** You will not be able to get a tight bend by hand, but most of the work can be done here. No heat is being used here, to show the cold-forming process, but a heat gun could be used if you remove the protective film before bending.

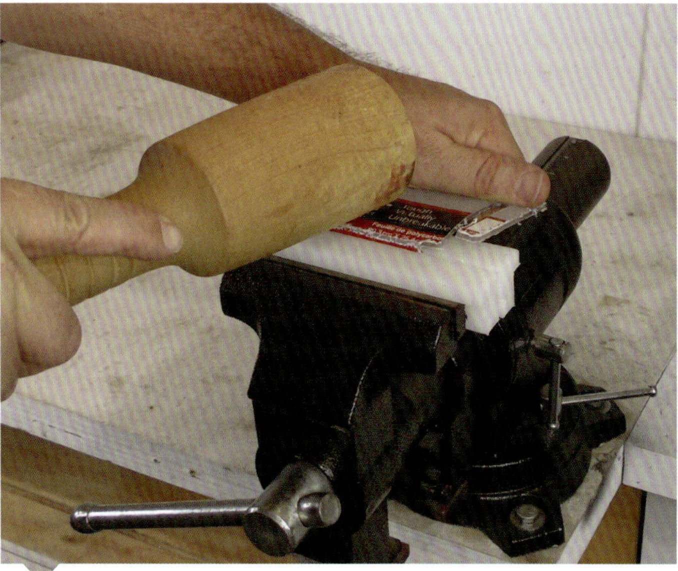

3. **Strike along the bend line to tighten the radius.** Get it as close to 90 degrees as possible. The bend will spring back a little bit when cold formed. This is normal and expected.

4. **Overbend the piece.** Remove the guard from the vise and reclamp it with the bend line above the jaws. Bend the guard beyond the 90-degree point and let it spring back. It should be closer to 90 degrees. Overbend it until the bend rests at 90 degrees after you let go. It will stay in this position.

5. **Remove the protective film.** You may see some wrinkles and strike marks in the bend from the cold forming and mallet, but it looks perfectly acceptable for a safety guard. Attach the hardware, and it is ready for the router table.

6.2 ICICLE ORNAMENT

Cold forming is mostly limited to thin polycarbonates. Generally, forming or bending plastic requires heating until it is soft enough to be formed without breaking. This icicle ornament is heated and twisted using an industrial heat gun. A torch like the one used for edge polishing in Chapter 4.2 can be used but will be harder to control.

Heating plastics carefully will soften them for fairly intricate forming.

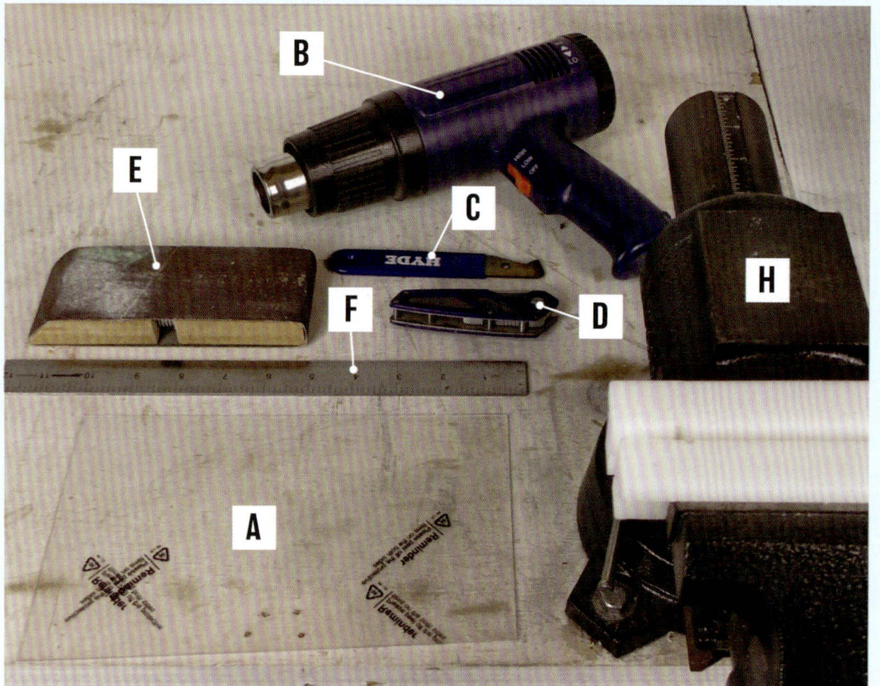

A heat gun is an excellent tool for general forming of plastics; a hair drier is not.

Supplies:

- A. Acrylic sheet, 0.06"–0.125" (1.5–3mm) thick
- B. Heat gun
- C. Scoring tool
- D. Utility knife
- E. Sanding block
- F. Ruler
- G. 1/8" (3mm) drill bit
- H. Vise
- I. Thermal gloves (optional)

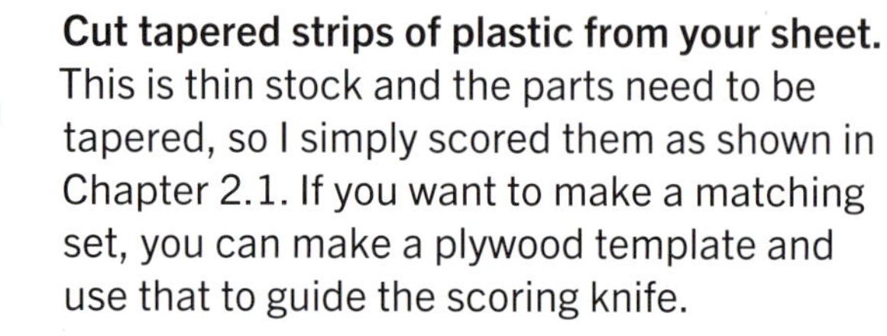

1. **Cut tapered strips of plastic from your sheet.** This is thin stock and the parts need to be tapered, so I simply scored them as shown in Chapter 2.1. If you want to make a matching set, you can make a plywood template and use that to guide the scoring knife.

2. **Snap the scored part from the sheet.** The material here is so thin that I found it easier to trap the part under the ruler and snap the sheet upward. This supports the fragile icicle, so it breaks cleanly along the entire score line. Use the utility knife to cut the back layer of protective film if needed.

Shape the ends of the tapers with a sanding block. I rounded over the top and left the bottom square, but you can design yours as you like. Remove the protective film, check the edges and clean up any issues.

3.

4. **Drill a small hole in the top of the icicle.** This is much easier to do when the part is flat. Support the icicle against a wood scrap to prevent chips or cracks as the bit exits the plastic. Use a wood backer so the bit is fully supported behind each hole.

5. **Form the twist in the icicle.** Clamp the tip into a vise or wood clamp and begin heating the strip with the heat gun. This plastic is very thin, so I found that a medium heat setting softened the plastic without it melting and distorting. Hold the part at the top using a glove if needed. You should be able to see the edges change slightly as the plastic reaches the right temperature. The snapped edge will melt slightly and become polished. Apply a very light twist to the plastic as you heat it, and you will be able to feel it begin to move under your fingers.

Work this part in stages. Complete one twist and let it cool before heating the next section and twisting it. It is best to begin by working slowly with lower heat. The parts can easily be heated more, but overheating usually results in ruined parts. This process does require practice. You will need to test the best settings for your heat gun with the plastic you are twisting. The actual twisting process needs a bit of skill as well. This is not difficult, but I threw away four or five of these before I learned the right technique.

6.

6.3 CARD HOLDER THERMOFORM

Before assembling the business card holder in Chapter 5.3, the body needs to be bent at a 90-degree angle to hold the cards. Most thermoforming of plastics is done through **strip bending**. This is the process of heating a narrow section of the plastic and then bending it along the line. This provides much more control than the heat gun we used for the icicle in Chapter 6.2. Most of the plastic is never heated, so it remains clean and undistorted.

This process does require a strip bender. I used to make simple ones using heating rope, but commercial units are now available cheap enough to justify having one in the shop for jobs like these. My strip bender uses a heating coil inside a glass tube to heat the plastic. This rests inside an aluminum extrusion. Water is pumped through the extrusion on each side of the heater to keep it cool over long use. This system creates a line or strip of heated plastic that is only about 3/8" (10mm) wide. The unheated parts are used to bend the heated strip into the angle needed.

The thermoformed bend in the body of this holder is more attractive than if it were made from two parts.

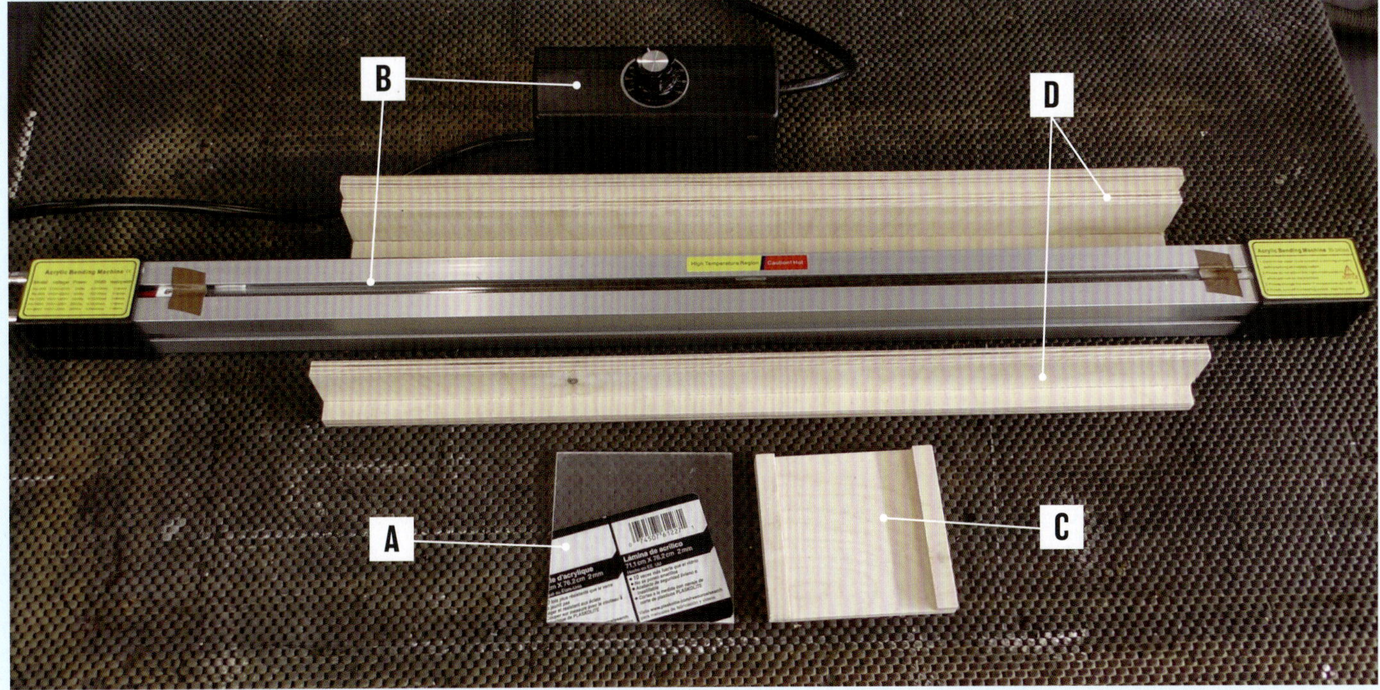

The strip bender is the main tool needed for this part of the project.

Supplies:

- **A.** 3-3/4" (95mm) x 4" (100mm) x 0.08" (2mm) acrylic body from Chapter 5.3
- **B.** Strip bender
- **C.** Cooling fixture (see sidebar on page 121)
- **D.** Support strips (optional)

1. **Peel away the protective film on the plastic part.** It cannot be over the heated area. On larger parts, the film can be left on except for about 1" (25mm) to each side of the heating area, but that is often more trouble than it is worth unless the parts need protection for shipping.

2. **Set the power on the strip bender control to about 75%.** Let it come up to full temperature. The heating element should be glowing a very dull orange. Bright is too hot. You will need to test your machine settings with scraps. More heat can be added, but too much can cause the plastic to bubble. Start at 75% and adjust as needed.

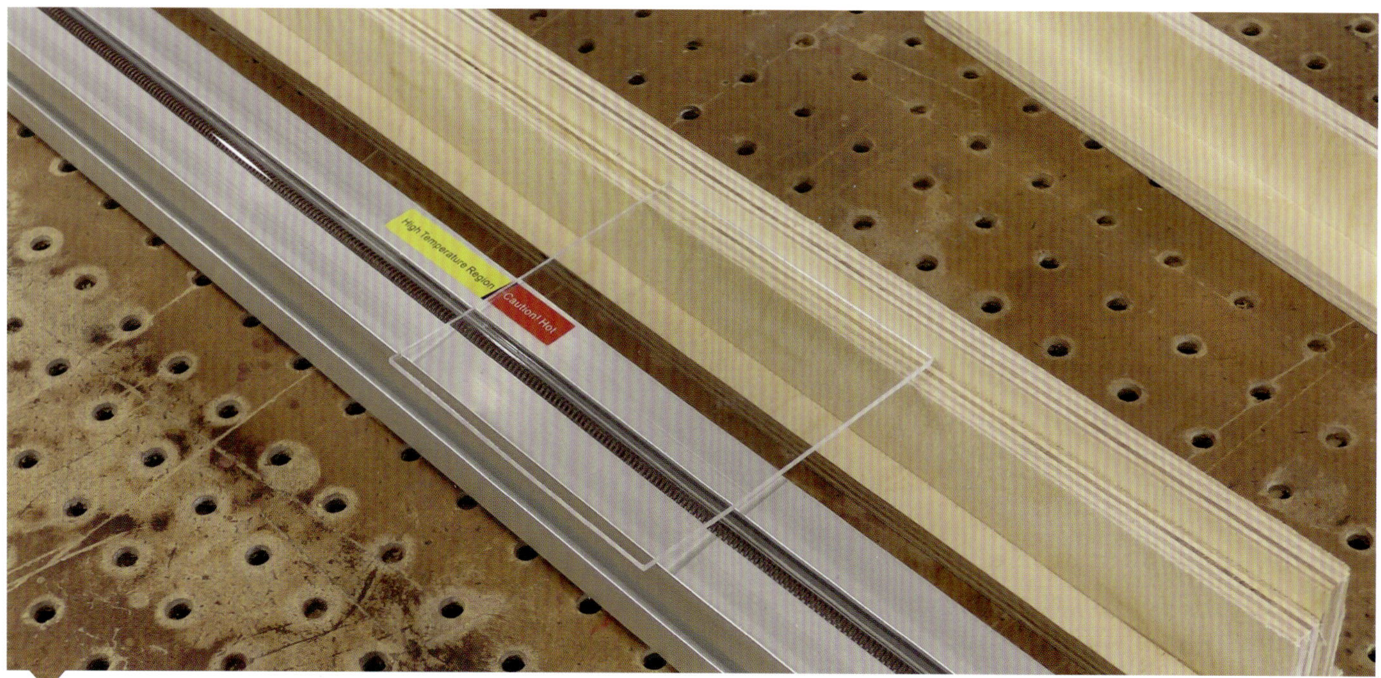

3. **Position the part onto the strip bender.** The center of the heat line should be 1" (25mm) away from one of the polished ends. Some strip benders have a support table and fence built in to locate the parts; this one does not, so I built a couple of support strips. Just T shapes that are the same height as the top of the bender will do. One of these has an additional plywood part that extends above the strip to act as a fence. This system is flexible enough to work with parts of all sizes.

4. **Flip the part every 20–30 seconds as it heats.** Be careful not to move the fence strip or touch the hot plastic to anything as you do. You should see the heated bend line distort the light compared to the unheated plastic, as shown. Look for a reflection of an overhead light on the heated area. As it gets closer, a round reflection will appear to stretch along the bend line. As you flip the part, you will be able to feel the heated strip bending when it is ready.

Lift the part off the heater and bend it to shape. The side that was last on the heater will be the hottest and softest. The cooler side should be inside the bend; this will provide the most attractive bend. The hot side will stretch slightly as it bends.

5.

Set the part into the cooling fixture. You can hold parts by hand until they cool, but simple shop-built cooling fixtures make more accurate parts. Be careful not to let the soft plastic touch anything that will mark it. Leave it in the fixture until it cools to prevent it from unbending.

6.

Cooling Fixture Geometry

Well-designed cooling fixtures allow for holding parts with multiple bends in the simplest manner possible.

When plastic is heated soft enough to bend, it is also soft enough to be marred if the hot section touches anything, so cooling fixtures need to be designed with this in mind. A simple L-shaped plywood fixture will keep the bend at 90 degrees until it is cool, but there is risk of marking the softened area. A gap at the corner can be added to mitigate this, but applying a little geometry to the problem offers an easier solution.

The body of the card holder is 3" (76mm) along the back and 1" (25mm) along the base. Think of these as two legs of a triangle, and we can determine the distance along the third side to be 3.16" (80mm) long. Setting two cleats at the right distance apart makes an easy cooling fixture.

The same trick works for the napkin holder (see Chapter 6.4) with the cleats set apart 2" (50mm), the same distance as the base bend. As long as the two bends are heated equally, the part will cool properly without elaborate fixturing.

6.4

NAPKIN HOLDER THERMOFORM

The napkin holder project we have been working on since Chapter 3 requires two bends instead of one. The first bend on this napkin holder would leave us with a 4" (100mm) "leg" on one side, but the bender is less than 2" (50mm) tall. It can be done, but it is not easy. Typically, it is easier to make multiple bends at the same time because the parts should be flipped as they heat for best results. So, we will set up two of the same machines from Chapter 6.3 to complete this bend.

These inexpensive strip benders are excellent for simple and occasional use. They are easy to set up and use, but they are limited in how close bends can be. Over the years, I have built production-sized bending tables that use nichrome ribbons to heat as many as a dozen bends at one time with as little as 3/4" (19mm) between. But that sort of system falls outside the "common woodworking tools" concept for this book.

The plastic part of this project needs two equal bends formed in it.

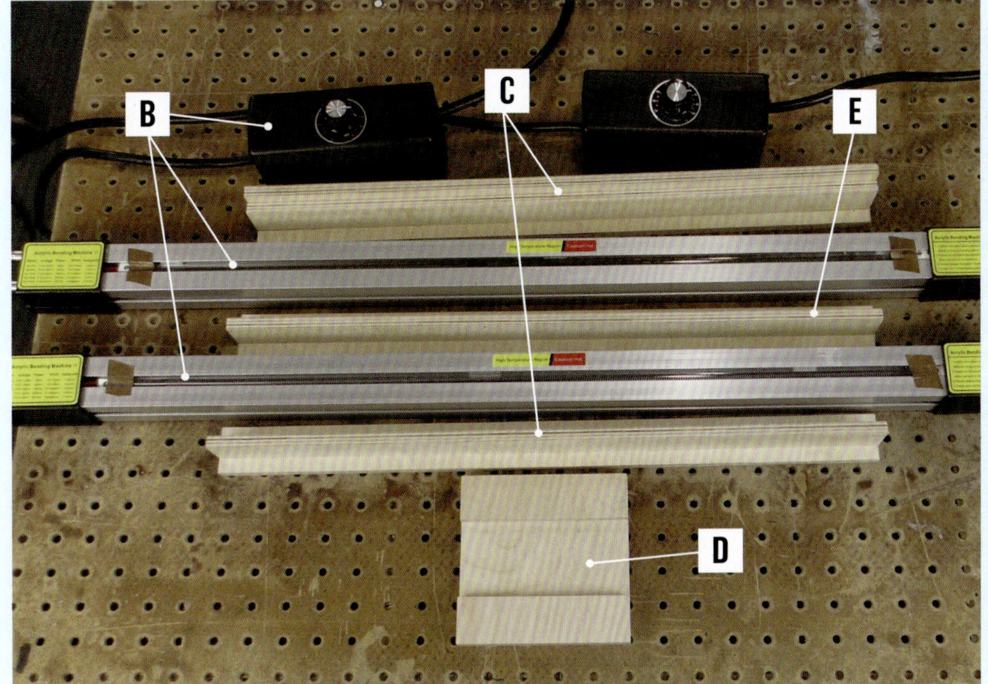

Multiple bends are usually easier to make at the same time.

Supplies:

- A. Acrylic napkin holder from Chapter 4.2
- B. Two strip bending machines
- C. Support strips
- D. Cooling fixture
- E. Spacer strip (optional)
- F. Infrared thermometer (optional)

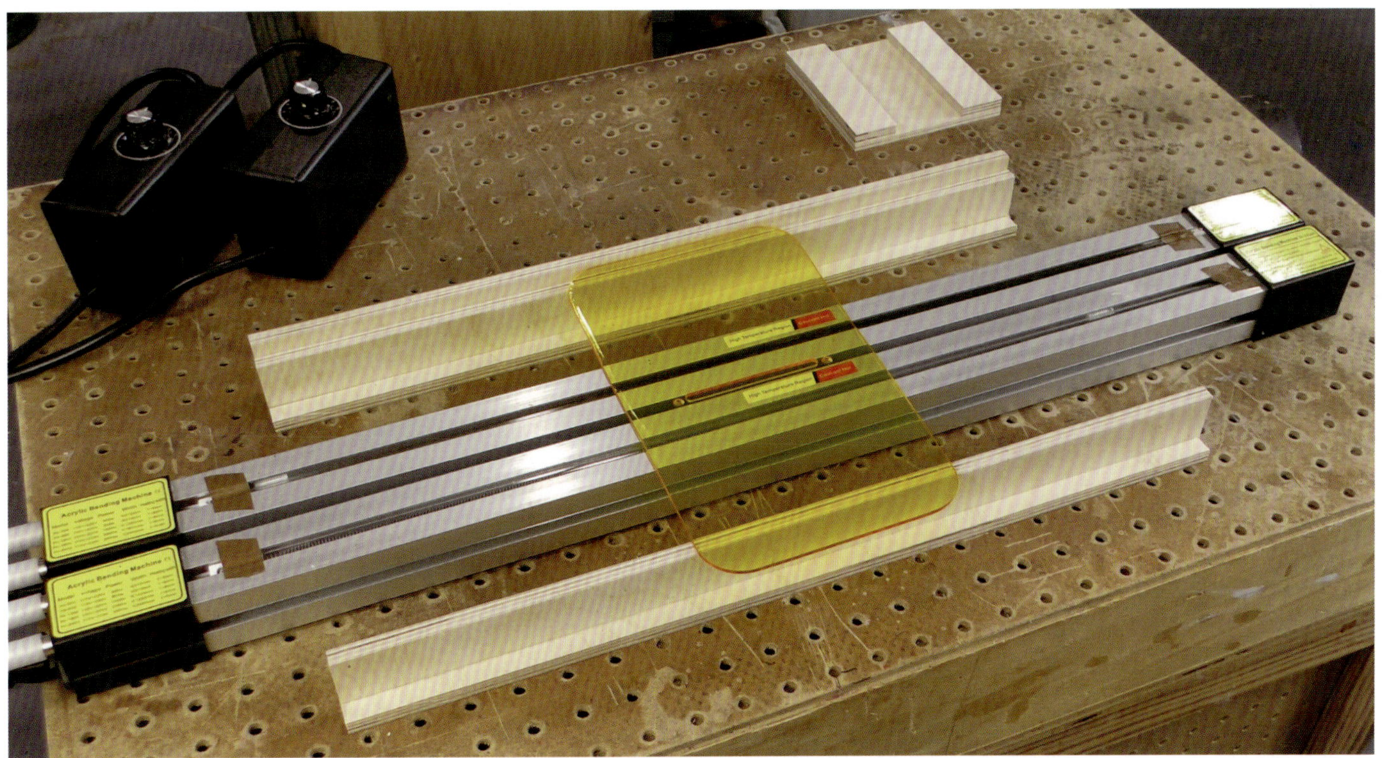

1. **Position the strip benders.** The heating elements should be parallel and 2" (50mm) apart center to center. The center slot should be parallel to the bends and centered between them. This should position the fence at 4" (100mm) from the center of the heating element. The fence will be very helpful in keeping the part aligned with the heaters as you work. If needed, you can use a spacer strip of plywood between the two heaters to keep them aligned. These units are limited to 2" (50mm) between them, so I designed the napkin holder to use that spacing. The support strips and fence can be positioned as well.

Turn on the heaters to about 75% and let them warm up. The two should be close in temperature, but I noticed with these that there was some difference, even though they are the same model. One had to be set to 85% to match the other. If you have an infrared thermometer, that will be helpful, but the color of the heating elements should be visually the same.

2.

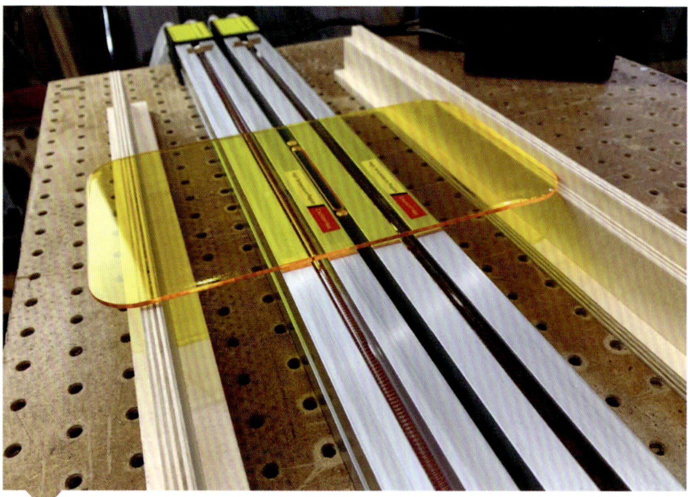

3. **Heat the acrylic.** Remove the protective film from the napkin holder blank and position it on the strip benders. Flip the part every 20 to 30 seconds. As the parts get close to bending temperature, you should be able to see two distinct lines in the plastic. Gently try to bend the part as you flip them. Don't force it; when ready, it will bend readily under your fingers.

4. **Remove the plastic from the heat.** Bend it into the U-shape needed. Be sure to bend the two sides away from the face that was last on the heat. This will provide a smoother and sharper bend. Set the bent part into the cooling fixture (see the sidebar in Chapter 6.3 for the dimensions). As long as the two bends are at equal temperature, the legs should stand straight in the cooling fixture without any other support.

Sources

Many common plastics can be found locally. Home centers and hardware stores typically have a selection of plastic sheets alongside the glass they carry for glazing. My local store also had a scoring knife along with the cleaner and polish I show in Chapter 5. A well-run hardware store may even cut parts to size for you.

Hobby stores often carry a selection of plastics, especially in ABS and styrene. Shops that specialize in radio-control cars or planes, trains, and model kits usually have a plastic display where you can find styrene sheets, rods, tubes, and other shapes. They may also stock the glues and accessories you need.

Most cities have at least one plastics distributor that stocks a huge variety of plastic sheets, rods, tubes, and other forms. They generally stock 4x8 sheets but will cut to size for a fee. These distributors will also carry the tools, glues, and accessories for plastics that you may need if you find yourself doing more plastic work.

It used to be that these distributors were the only real option for getting anything other than plastic sheets for glazing, but the internet now offers any number of options if you do not have one in your area.

Acrylic shapes, hinges, latches, and other accessories can be hard to find even online. The folks at Lustercraft are helpful and happy to serve everyone, not just businesses. Their information can be found below:

Lustercraft Plastics
1818 S Meridian Ave
Wichita, KS 67213
800-362-2492
lustercraft.com

Your local Woodcraft Supply carries UHMW sheet stock in various thicknesses and in tape form for applying where needed. These items are also available at Woodcraft.com.

Rockler Stores across the US carry acrylic sheets for router and saw bases as well as UHMW in sheets and tapes of various sizes. They are also available online at Rockler.com

Index

Note: Page numbers in *italics* indicate projects.

About the Author

Ralph Bagnall has been working in the wood and plastics industries for nearly 40 years. The founder of Consulting Woodworker, a company specializing in physical plant consulting, video production, and marketing services for the woodworking industry, Ralph also hosts *Woodcademy TV*, where he teaches tips, tricks, and techniques that woodworkers of all skill levels can apply in their shops.

His written work has been published in national magazines, including *Woodworker's Journal, Woodcraft*, and *Woodshop News*. He is also a frequent speaker at prominent woodworking events, such as the International Woodworking Fair, National Wood Flooring Association Show, and The International Surfaces Exhibition. To learn more about Ralph, visit www.Woodcademy.com.